To Ron —
Best Always

Don't Make Me Cry, Roy

Adventures In Interviewing

Roy Firestone
With Scott Ostler
Foreword by Rick Reilly

Published by Magic Turtle Press

Magic Turtle Press • PO Box 56927. Sherman Oaks, CA 91413

Don't make me cry, roy /
by Roy Firestone with Scott Ostler -- 1st ed.

p.   cm.

978-0-9801122-0-7   0-9801122-0-6

Book Design and Production by
JK NAUGHTON

Jacket design by
Robert Evans

Cover photography
© Roy Firestone

W W W . R O Y F I R E S T O N E . C O M

Don't Make Me Cry, Roy

Adventures In Interviewing

Roy Firestone

With Scott Ostler

Foreword by Rick Reilly

Roy Firestone has interviewed more than 5,000 famous athletes and entertainers on television, and he has zero kills to his credit.

Roy doesn't attack, he converses, connects and communicates with his guests, providing the viewer with rare glimpses into their hearts and souls. Now, in this his second book, Roy takes you behind the interviews and inside the circus of sport, with his thoughts, opinions and observations of the people with whom he has interacted over the last 30 years.

Firestone brings you personal anecdotes of such figures as Ted Williams, Barry Bonds, Bobby Knight, Magic Johnson, Alex Rodriguez, Tom Cruise, Michael Vick, Mark Cuban...and even a few sane people.

Read hilarious tales of Roy helping Cuba Gooding Jr. win an Oscar; almost having his career ruined by Bobby Knight; facing a near-death experience with Albert Belle; and encountering white-knuckle stage fright while singing the National Anthem before 60,000 football fans.

Roy swears he never tries to make anyone cry, so you might want to skip the heart-tugging chapters on Dikembe Mutombo, Christopher Reeve, Bill Walton and Troy Aikman. And be warned that emotions are involved throughout the book. You'll be amazed and amused, and you might be surprised at Roy's take on such "dangerous dudes" as Warren Sapp and Ray Lewis.

Take this guided tour through Roy Firestone's world as he reveals his all-time favorite interview subjects, his (shorter) list of buffoons and jerks, and his lists of pet peeves and of reasons why he just can't quit.

It's a box of chocolates for the sports fan's soul, offered up from the heart, and from the best seat in the house.

FOREWORD
By Rick Reilly

I told Roy Firestone, "You're not going to make me cry, Roy."

But he did, he made me cry when he told me he wasn't going to pay me to write this forward.

I wrote it anyway, for three reasons:

One: Maybe he'll change his mind and pay me.

Two: Maybe he'll at least buy me dinner some time. Lunch? Maybe a bagel at Jerry's?

Three: Roy is the best interviewer there is, and as a former Cub Scout den leader, I'm sworn to tell the truth.

Roy can nail a great interview without even raising his voice, threatening, sneak-attacking, goading, wheedling, insulting or otherwise provoking & inciting his subject.

In other words, he is a dinosaur, and that's a compliment, because I'm not referring to Roy's wardrobe or the size of his brain.

My guess is that Roy wasn't paying attention at Interview School when they taught that you're supposed to treat your subject as if he or she were tied to the chair in the basement of the old precinct house, under the 250-watt heat lamp.

Roy's interviews are interesting conversations, not gory bullfights.

But why take my word for it? The wisest and most-insightful person I ever ran into in my business, sportswriting, was the late L.A. Times columnist Jim (Pulitzer Prize) Murray, and he wrote this: "Roy Firestone is the best interviewer I ever saw. That's not sports interviewer. That's interviewer, period. That includes Mike Wallace, Barbara Walters, Diane Sawyer, Morley Safer. Any and all of the above."

Here's a little more of what Murray wrote:

"Interviewing is a high and holy art. It is not the confrontational thrusting of a microphone under the lips of an accused as he steps out of his car at the office, it is not framing questions to show how clever you are. It is a tactic to elicit information, shed light on the personality of the interviewee. It calls for its practitioner to be adroit, curious, emphatic, multi-ranged and sensitive."

Wow. Therefore, by the power that ought to be vested in me, I bestow upon Roy Firestone the same honor that I once heard a basketball player say should be bestowed on a sportswriter. The player said, "They should give him the Wurlitzer Prize."

An extra organ can be very handy, you know.

For me, a Roy Firestone interview is great television, because I know I'm going to be entertained and I'm going to learn something about the personality of the person with whom he's having a conversation and not have to suffer from some Mr. Blowdry America preening into the camera and telling me all about himself and nothing about the guest; or some brain-bruised ex-jock on the sideline who can't even think of a question and instead simply blurts, "Tank, talk about the game." Oy.

What Roy does is connect with people. That's his trick, his gimmick. My only complaint is that my television set should show more of him and less of the guys who haven't given the art of conversation the first thought.

Okay, I said all that nice stuff. And it's all true. But can I at least have a free copy of the book?

Charlie and Lucy Wedemeyer

Real heroes in our midst.

chapter 1

WHY SPORTS MATTER

"There are stubborn and unknown souls who defend themselves inch by inch in the shadows, against the fatal invasion of want and turpitude. They are noble and mysterious triumphs, which no eye sees, no renowned rewards and no flourish of trumpets salutes. Life, misfortune, isolation, abandonment and poverty are battlefields which have their heroes."
– Victor Hugo

Do sports matter?

To me, they do. They have provided me with a pretty good living, and a pretty good life.

But how about in the greater scheme?

Is it all just perspiration, or is there also inspiration?

I admit that a lot of the games are just games, and a lot of the players are unremarkable.

But there are moments when it all makes sense, when sports become something bigger and more important than trophies, stats, rotisserie leagues and tailgate parties.

The moments are made by people, and it's the *people* that I find compelling, intriguing, entertaining and, at their best, truly inspirational. That's what it's all about for me – the people.

I'm going to tell you three quick stories of people I've met through my sports job. A coach, a priest and a politician.

First, the coach. When you talk about the great football coaches, you talk Rockne and Lombardi, Bill Walsh and Tom Landry. But number one on my list, hands down, is Charlie Wedemeyer. You haven't heard of Charlie? Los Gatos High School in Northern California?

Charlie played at Michigan and was a good player, but at 5'7" and 160 he was way too small for the NFL, so he became a high school coach, and a good one. Charlie was giving a chalk talk one day in 1977 when the chalk slipped out of his hand. He picked up the chalk, started to write and the chalk fell again. This kind of stuff kept happening, but he felt fine otherwise and assumed it was some minor nerve damage from his playing days. Finally he underwent testing, and was told he had amyotrophic lateral sclerosis – Lou Gehrig's Disease.

It's a disease and a death sentence. As nerves controlling muscles die out, parts of the body, one after another and in no set pattern, shut down forever, until nothing works. Charlie was 30. His doctor gave him three years to live, tops.

Charlie coached Los Gatos High for seven more years. The Los Gatos Wildcats won a division championship with coach Wedemeyer calling the game from his wheelchair. As this is written Charlie is 58 years old, he can't speak, can't breathe without a respirator. But he can smile, and he has as full and meaningful a life as anyone I know.

His wife Lucy learned to read lips and she is Charlie's speaker. She refers to ALS as "our disease." Charlie has become something of a philosopher, motivational "speaker" and general beacon of humanity. He is in constant pain and he lives to give others hope.

"Death is a conclusion," Charlie says. "It doesn't matter how or when you die, what matters is how you live until you die."

He also says, "There are people on this planet who are living to die. I feel like I'm dying to live."

While others fear growing old or failing to realize career goals, Charlie has simpler fears. Falling. Choking on his food. His strength is not just a religious faith. He said, "Pain and suffering are inevitable, but misery is optional."

I saw Charlie speak to a group of football players in Seattle. A massive linebacker stood up, tears streaming down his face, and said to Charlie, "I just want to come up there and give you a hug." And he did.

Charlie has a tremendous emotional impact on everyone he comes in contact with, including the many disadvantaged high school athletes who are awarded college scholarships through Charlie's foundation.

When he says, "We're all terminal," the words hit home. You can't be around Charlie Wedemeyer and not gain a greater appreciation for life.

I did a program once years ago on Verbum Dei High School in Los Angeles. The basketball coach, Father James, had done a remarkable job of taking at-risk inner-city kids and not only turning them into fine basketball players, but motivating them to become top students and citizens. Inspiring them.

Father James told me a story.

"A boy and his grandfather are walking in a valley, the little boy falls over a rock and says, 'Oh, crap!' And he hears his own echo. He's never heard an echo before, he's fascinated, and he tries it again. 'You're an idiot!' he yells. 'I hate you!'

"His grandfather taps the boy on the shoulder and tells him to listen, then the grandfather shouts out, 'I love you! You're terrific! You're a champion! I feel good!'

"The boy says, 'What are you doing, grandpa?' The grandfather says, 'Life is an echo. Everything we do in our lives has to do with what we put out. If we put out hatred and resentment and anger, that's what we get back, time after time. If you want love, you need to put out love, if you want more confidence, you put out confidence. Life is an echo.'"

This book, if it's about anything, is about people who are not only interesting and athletically talented, but who inspire.

I believe in positive vibes, a belief that was reinforced by James Carville, one of President Clinton's advisors and a savvy politician. I've gotten to know Carville pretty well, he's a likeable and intelligent guy, but I really came to appreciate him the night we were both part of a program in Bakersfield.

It's two weeks after 9/11, and there are 9,000 people in the arena, and the program includes astronaut/senator John Glenn, Arnold Schwarzenegger and former British Prime Ministers John Major and Margaret Thatcher.

I give my presentation, and then Bill O'Reilly of Fox TV steps to the microphone. O'Reilly is on fire, he preaches about how we have to close our borders to foreigners, ship Muslims back to the Mideast, tap phones, give America back to Americans. O'Reilly has the crowd in a frenzy. Even though it's California, this is very conservative middle America, and nerves are still raw from 9/11.

The format of the program is a debate. After O'Reilly, it's Carville's turn, and he walks into a lion's den. The crowd is hissing and booing before he says a word.

Carville says, "I'm not going to debate whether or not we should close our borders or whatnot. I'd just like to tell you a story told to me by a priest in Baton Rouge. It's a story of two men in a Nazi concentration camp. One of the men is dying, he's emaciated, barely able to speak. He has been brutalized and tortured, has lost his entire family. He is praying, and he has a smile on his face.

"His friend, who is close to death himself, says, 'Moishe, why are you smiling?' Moishe says, 'I'm smiling as I speak to God.' The other guy says, 'Speak to God? The God who has allowed your life to come to this? Who has allowed your family to he murdered, and has brought you near death? What can you be asking this God for?' Moishe says, 'Oh, I'm not asking him for anything.' 'Then why are you talking to him?' 'I'm giving thanks.' 'Giving thanks? Look at us! The Nazis have destroyed us. How can you be giving thanks?'

"Moishe points across the camp to some marching Nazis and says, 'I'm smiling and giving thanks to my God that I'm not one of them.'"

Suddenly the arena is absolutely quiet. Carville says, "The effect is this: There is nothing comparable to the Holocaust. And if above that event can rise such a spirit, what else can we not rise above? The importance and the beauty is always greater than the hideousness and the hatred, Always. More than that, the bigger point, is if we allow ourselves to lose our values and our democracy, take away the opportunities and freedoms in the pursuit of hatred, we have become them."

I've never seen anything like this. On a story, on a simple appeal to tolerance, the crowd has completely turned, their hearts have melted.

"We have an obligation to forgive others for acts and crimes of intolerance," Carville says, "even though the desire is to hate, and the visceral feeling is for revenge. If you do not embrace the concept of forgiveness, mankind will never advance. We have to be better. We have to look at the goodness and the greatness in our lives."

That's what sports allow me to do, to look at goodness and greatness. To me, sports matter.

With Cameron Crowe, Cuba Gooding, Jr., and Tom Cruise

I taught 'em everything I know about making movies.

With Cuba Gooding, Jr.

The tears are about to flow.

chapter

2

"DON'T MAKE ME CRY, ROY!"

In my quarter century in the TV sports business I've conducted more than 5,000 interviews, and if there is one quality I strive for in each session it is sincerity. Be real.

So what interview am I best known for? The one I faked.

Not only that, the guy I interviewed was faking, and he was rewarded for his insincere sincerity with the highest honor in his business, the Academy Award.

It started one morning in 1996 when the phone rang in the office of *Up Close*, the daily ESPN program I was hosting. My producer, Jason Schirn, answered the phone.

The caller identified herself as a casting person working with movie director Cameron Crowe.

"We're looking for a Roy Firestone-type guy for a movie," the woman said.

"What about Roy Firestone?" Jason suggested, helpfully.

"Hmm. Do you think you could help us get in touch with him?"

"I think I could do that," Jason told her, handing me the phone.

The woman told me Crowe was working on a movie to be titled *Jerry Maguire*, about a sports agent. The title role would be played by Tom Cruise.

"Do you know anything about sports agents?" the casting woman asked me.

I told her I knew a little. I didn't tell her that a movie about a sports agent didn't sound very exciting.

The woman said, "The star athlete in the movie is going to go on a TV talk show. We were watching your show the other night and you had Dennis Rodman on, and he was crying. Was that real?"

I laughed. I guess movie people assume everything on TV is scripted, like a wrestling match.

"Yeah, it was pretty much real," I said.

"Unbelievable!" she said. "Do you think we could get you and Dennis Rodman to be in this movie?"

They were considering casting Dennis Rodman as Jerry Maguire's star-athlete client.

"I think it would be a huge mistake for you to have Dennis Rodman play a major part with Tom Cruise," I said. "Huge."

"Well, we have other actors in mind, too," she said. "Would you be interested in playing yourself in a small cameo?"

"Sure."

From that moment until I arrived at the studios for the filming, I went on Hollywood automatic pilot. As in: Been here, done this. It's not that I'm jaded or cool, it's just that I know when someone offers me a small cameo role, it's probably going to be so small it's invisible. And I'll be playing myself, which I've done in maybe 15 different movies and TV shows, so I've pretty much got me down.

One of the perks of my job is a certain visibility in Hollywood. I get these little acting parts, they're easy, they're usually fun, I get a nice check, and once in a great while my entire scene does not wind up on the cutting-room floor. If my part survives the original edit and my microcameo is on the screen, it invariably gets cut in the later versions, when the movie is shortened for TV. So let's just say I don't take myself overly-serious as an actor.

I played myself in *Juwanna Mann* with Vivica A. Fox, in *The Scout* with Albert Brooks, in a Muhammad Ali movie titled *The Greatest*. I've been on *Everybody Loves Raymond* several times.

Okay, it's kind of fun to do TV and movie work, and when my filming day for *Jerry Maguire* came I was honestly excited about meeting Tom Cruise, whom I consider to be a very talented actor.

Crowe's people had sent me the script, of course, but I never opened it. I prepare thoroughly for my real interviews, but in this case, why bother? I ain't DeNiro gaining 30 pounds and getting my game face on for *Raging Bull*. I'm Roy preparing to be Roy, reciting a few easy lines.

Months later I confessed to Cameron Crowe that I hadn't looked at the script. He said, "Thanks a lot, Roy."

When I arrive on the set at Sony Studios in Century City, it's lunchtime. The first person I see is Tom Cruise, who rushes up to welcome me.

"Roy, what a great pleasure! I can't believe you're doing the movie, thank you so much!"

I would have spit out my coffee had I been drinking coffee. Sometimes I almost have to laugh at the unreal situations my work puts me into. Tom Cruise is thanking *me* for being in his movie. Shouldn't it be the other way around? Oh well.

Cruise is hanging out with a little kid, playing some kind of made-up ball game. They're getting along so well that I assume the boy is Cruise's adopted son. Wrong, it's Jonathan Lipnicki, who plays the little boy in the movie. But not having read the script, I don't know that there's a kid in the movie.

Cruise, by the way, cannot be more gracious, to everyone. He hangs with all the other actors and crew, eats with 'em, sits in on everyone else's scenes, offers encouragement, just gives the whole movie-making process a real team feeling.

I walk onto the set for my scene, and it is freaky. The producers originally wanted to film the scene on our regular set, but ESPN wouldn't grant permission, for some reason. So the prop people have re-created my entire interview studio, meticulously, down the monitors and background equipment, which won't even be on-camera. It's like walking in to a hotel room in Des Moines and finding it's an exact replica of your own living room, down to the magazines on your coffee table.

A pleasant fellow approaches me, offers his hand and says, "Roy? Cuba!"

I smile, shake his hand and ask, "Uh, what *about* Cuba?"

"No," he says, "*I'm* Cuba. Cuba Gooding Jr."

Oops. I have no idea who Cuba Gooding is. For all I know he's the caterer. I don't see a lot of movies or watch a lot of TV, other than sports. I have seen Gooding in *A Few Good Men*, but the association doesn't click in when he introduces himself.

Incidentally, I did the same thing with Ray Romano. The first time I worked on his show, it was new, and I wasn't even aware of the show's name. Ray introduced himself: "Hey, Roy, I'm Ray Romano."

Romano is a very talented guy, but he doesn't look like a big star, which is part of his charm. I had no idea who he was. I said, "Hi, Ray, nice to meet you. What do you do with the show?"

The show's co-star, Peter Boyle, was standing there and he got this oh-my-God frozen smile on his face, and he said, "Roy? Ray doesn't work *with* the show. He IS the show."

I laughed and played it off like a joke.

"I'm just kidding!" I chuckled. "I *know* who *Ray Romano* is."

Thus I narrowly avoided being thrown off the set for disrespecting the star.

Anyway, I pull the same lame stunt with Cuba Gooding, but he is also a very nice fellow and doesn't take offense.

Next, Cuba and I huddle with Cameron Crowe, whom I already know, to talk about the scene.

"Okay, Roy," Cameron says, "the scene is you and Cuba, of course, and I want you guys to kind of ad lib the dialogue. You know the story."

"Sure," I say, "but, uh, just refresh me a bit."

"Okay. Cuba's character, Rod Tidwell, has waited his entire career to finally get a big contract. During an earlier scene Tidwell watches your program when your interview subject breaks down and cries, and Tidwell says to his agent, 'Everybody cries on this show.' Like it's so uncool.

"So in this scene you start doing your Roy Firestone thing, talking about his life, about his mom and dad, and about all the people who have failed him. You're trying to make him cry. And he won't cry, until you tell him he's got this huge new contract. Got it? Just adlib."

Cuba and I talk briefly. He tells me he doesn't know much about sports. He says, "When football players are on your show, how do they act? How do they sit?"

I tell him they're usually cocky, they kind of don't give me much eye contact. So here I am, giving acting tips to Cuba Gooding.

No rehearsal. We do two takes. Boom, boom, done.

I am not aware during the filming that Cruise has taken Gooding aside and told him that once he starts crying, really let it go, just wail, then leap over the table and grab Roy and bear-hug him. Had I known, I would have demanded a stunt double.

Take One... I let it fly off the top of my head, doing a satire of a Roy Firestone interview.

Me (solemnly, to Tidwell):

Your father leaves home on Christmas Eve, leaving your family all alone. Your mother has to sweep the steps of the prison just to earn enough for your tuition. Your brother loses a leg in a tragic bass-fishing accident. There's been a horrific list of things that happened to you.

Tidwell (stubbornly):

I'm not gonna cry, Roy!

Me:

Well, actually we have some very good news for you. This has just been handed to me, a memo, it's signed, it's a contract, guaranteed, Arizona Cardinals, four years, 11-point-2 million dollars. You get to play in Arizona where it all started, finish up your career in Arizona. Whattaya think of that?

Cuba starts crying. Real tears, incidentally, which shocks me. Now he's sobbing, and suddenly he leaps across the table and pounces on me. We've got these cheap office chairs on casters, and the two of us fall backwards, almost off the set.

It's hysterical, everyone is laughing, but I think it surprised the camera people. So we do it again.

Take Two... Same deal, real tears again, Tidwell leaps the table, hugs Roy, this time without the chair crash.

Cut. Print. Whatever.

I'm kind of jazzed. I realize the scene probably won't make the final edit (extensive scenes featuring my ESPN colleagues Chris Berman and Dan Patrick would get edited out). But hey, I get to hang out on the set with Tom Cruise, Renee Zellweger, Troy Aikman, Katarina Witt. Cruise asks to have his picture taken with me. I get a check for three or four grand, it's a hoot.

Then I go back to the real world and completely forget about the movie. Seriously, what kind of fuss could there be over a movie about a sports agent?

About a year later I get a phone call from a friend, Larry Grobel, and he's out of breath.

"Roy, Roy! Oh, my god, oh my god!"

"What is it, Larry?"

"Jerry Maguire! Unbelievable!"

"Who's Jerry Maguire?"

"The movie, Roy, *Jerry Maguire*! Remember?"

"Oh, you mean the Tom Cruise thing I did a year ago? Did I survive the cut?"

"Did you survive the *cut*? You're the whole payoff of the movie! They'll never be able to edit you out of the Late Movie version, never! You're the inside joke that ties everything together at the end!"

"No way."

"Way! And this guy Cuba Gooding is fabulous. He might even get an Academy Award nomination."

"Yeah, Cuba, I remember him."

The next morning at 11 o'clock, I'm the first person in line at the Universal City multiplex. It's so early that they're sweeping up the popcorn from the previous night. It's the second day of *Jerry Maguire* and I'm the only person in the theatre.

I'm blown away. It's a funny scene, Cuba is great, our scene is a key element in the movie. I'm like a little kid watching myself in a movie.

Fast-forward six months, the Academy Award nominations are announced and guess who's up for Best Supporting Actor? No, not Roy. Cuba! And the night of the Awards, when they show movie clips of each nominee, the clip they show for Cuba is the scene he did with me. Crazy.

What's crazier is that the movie never goes away. Every day it happens. I'll be in a supermarket or airport and a stranger will yell to me, "I'm not gonna CRY, Roy! You're not gonna make me CRY!" I always laugh.

And famous people. Arnold Schwarzenegger, Barry Bonds, Bob Dole, Jeff Gordon, they all lay it on me. It's not, "Hi, Roy, nice to meet you." It's, "I'm not gonna CRY, Roy."

In my 5,000-plus interviews over the years, I've "made" about 25 guys cry. Those are the interviews people remember the most. They say, "I saw the show where Rodman cried." Or Bonds. Or George Brett. "Magic cried on your show!"

People think all I do is lure famous athletes on my show and make 'em cry. That's why the joke in the movie is so perfect, because people remember the tears.

A few years after we made the movie I ran into Cuba Gooding at a fight in Las Vegas. He came up to me and he didn't say hello. He said, "You got me the Academy Award!"

I almost cried.

Bill Walton

Ted Walton's lucky old son.

FATHERS AND SONS

The interview is a form of storytelling. If I do my homework, and pay attention to my subject, my questions will help tell the story. It's almost like I can tee it up, but the guest has to hit the ball.

Two of my favorite interview subjects are Bill Walton and Hubie Brown, and two of my favorite interviews involved Bill and Hubie telling stories, from the heart.

I interviewed Brown the day he was inducted into the Basketball Hall of Fame, honored for his coaching career. Hubie knows basketball at a genius level, so I did ask him some basketball questions, but not many.

Some critics say I don't ask enough of the balls-and-bats questions, because that's what the sports fans really want to hear. Sorry, I can't go that way. I'm not a sports expert. I realized long ago that if I have a contribution to make to the interview form, it's in shedding a ray of light into a person's soul, exposing a bit of what makes them tick, what drove them to greatness. When I can do that, tears or not, I'm happy, and I believe viewers are, too.

Hubie Brown is one of my favorite guests for two reasons. One, he is an historical figure in basketball, he has been associated with more famous people than Forrest Gump. Two, Hubie is an absolute fountain of emotional honesty. Even what may have sounded like corny throwaway cliché turned into a heartfelt expression of appreciation for his wife.

I reminded Brown of the time we had run into one another one day in Paris, in the Louvre. It was 1985, and back in the States the NBA Finals was in progress, a Lakers-Celtics classic, and everyone remotely associated with the NBA was watching – except Hubie, there with his wife in the Louvre, because he was "keeping my wife happy."

Someone else might have left it there, you know, "You gotta keep the little woman happy." Not Hubie. He turned it into a tribute.

"Your wife," he said, "is the one that has to make the sacrifices. She's the one that's got to uproot all of the furnishings, worry about the children, move to another city. You (the coach) get to the new city, you already have friendships. Not all of your children's personalities are the same and they will get a feel of how they should react from the boss of the house, which is the wife. She has got to make it work."

Hubie talked about how over the years he uprooted his wife and family 10 times to change coaching jobs. He talked about the hardest move, the first one, when he left his high school coaching-teaching job for an assistant coaching job at William & Mary.

"I'm making $18,750 at Fairlawn High School," Hubie said. "I was teaching seniors business law, coaching basketball, and then I was assistant coach for football and baseball, I was running a swim club in the summer time, life is beautiful, everybody is happy. The kids think you're God, right? Your wife has all these friends. Then William & Mary offers me a job for $7,000. So I was sitting on the campus of William & Mary at two in the morning and I'm saying to a friend, 'How can I do this?' I mean, to go from $18,750 back to $7,000!

"When I went home and I presented the package (to his wife), she said, 'Let's go.'"

So already the viewer has learned that we're not dealing with a garden-variety man, wife, or relationship.

Earlier that day I attended Hubie's induction ceremony, and afterwards I listened to him speak fondly of his late father, Charlie Brown. So in the interview I asked Brown to talk about his father and the challenges he faced, making it through life on a third-grade education.

Hubie sighed, looked at the ceiling and said, "You know how to make a man cry, don't you?"

He paused briefly and continued.

"I have difficulty talking about my father without getting extremely emotional, because he was a giant. When he lost his job after the Second World War – he was a foreman in the shipyards – he walked the streets for eight months, and then he became my (high) school's janitor for $50 a week, six days a week. He stayed there until I completed ninth through 12th grades, until I went to college.

"He would tell me, 'No matter how good you think you got it, no matter how good you are, at the top of your game always remember you're a half a step from the street.'"

Hubie and his dad called one another "Chief," and they were very close. Hubie played baseball and basketball in college and never stopped hearing from his father.

"He was demanding because he knew that this (sports) is how we were going to get out (of poverty) and I was going to be able to move on, and excellence was pounded, and by that I mean never short-changing the coach, never short-changing your teammates, always the team is bigger than the individual."

I told Hubie I had been struck earlier that day with the pain on his face when he talked about his parents.

"My father never made a hundred dollars (a week)," he said, and he stopped, and gulped, and leaned his head back to keep the tears from falling.

"Would you like to stop?" I asked him. Normally we don't stop taping during an interview except for a technical problem, but I knew it had been an emotional day for Hubie and I didn't want to put him in an embarrassing spot.

He didn't acknowledge my question, because he never heard me. He was gone. Or rather, I was gone, and the cameras and lights were gone, and Hubie was back in the old neighborhood with his father. As the tears fell, Hubie went right on talking.

"He had an icebox on the back porch. When you travel on the railroad from New York to Newark to Washington, our apartments were right up against those railroad tracks. Those trains put you to sleep at night. In the winter the heat went to only two rooms. The other two rooms the heat never reached. But you know what? I never wanted to grow up any other way, because everything you got you earned.

"I served mass at St. Elizabeth's Hospital every morning from the fifth grade until the day I went to college, from 6:30 to 7. We'd go into that hospital and give out communion and then I was able to eat breakfast with the doctors. I needed that dollar a week (for serving mass) and I needed that breakfast. Sister Patrick, this nun, beautiful woman, used to take care of me, she watched me grow. To this day they're my number-one charity, the Sisters of Charity.

"One day we (Hubie and some pals) decided to go to the downtown area. We went to Woolworth's and we picked up (shoplifted) a few things we should not have picked up. My father came home at 5:30. I'll never forget this. He said, 'What's that?' I said, 'It's a pencil-sharpener.' He said, 'Where did you get it?' I said, 'I got it at Woolworth's.' He said, 'How much did it cost?' I said, 'Two cents,' and he said, 'Where did you get the money?'

"And he knew that I had stolen that pencil sharpener. He grabbed me, he got my jacket and put it on me, we went down the back stairs, down into the street, all the way to Woolworth's. I'm shaking the whole time, he was crushing me. Into Woolworth's. He took me right there to the counter. He took out the pencil sharpener and gave it to the woman and gave her two cents. The most humiliating day of my entire life. I never stole again. That was my old man. The lessons I got from him were the best. I never cheated an employer, never cheated a player, never cheated a coach who was out there listening to me at a clinic. I never cheated that family that's listening to the television, I tried to educate them and give them my heart every day."

That was one day I was glad I didn't devote the entire interview to asking Hubie to explain the pick-and-roll.

Here's another disclaimer: If I knew when I was going to make a guest cry, I'd try to build the show around that. With Bill Walton, the tears came near the end of our interview, so we almost missed out on the best part.

Like Hubie Brown, Walton is almost alarmingly honest, but if you know him only from his TV commentating, you might think of him as sort of a knowledgeable goofball. I find him to not only to be a kind of hippie-era Renaissance man, but also a guy with a lot of depth and very open, but in previous interviews we'd never gotten to any real emotional places.

I went to his home in San Diego for the interview, and it's a crazy place, a hodgepodge tribute to the Grateful Dead, Native Americans, and John Wooden. And I noticed on the wall several notes and letters about his father, who died not long before. Near the end of the long interview, I asked him about his dad.

Roy:

We have just a couple moments left and I wanted to take the opportunity to read a couple things to you. This is an obituary from July 23, 2004, and this is the first paragraph. "Any child of William T. (Ted) Walton knew the family right of passage- play musical instruments, play sports, study hard in school. As the patriarch of the family known for its athletes, Mr. Walton was the musical maestro. He sang bass, he played piano and about half a dozen other instruments. And on and on.

Walton:

So many stories, Roy. He was the most un-athletic person I've ever seen. I never shot a single basket with my dad. I saw him run one time, at the church picnic, and I fell over laughing. But he taught us everything. He taught us about love. He taught us about family, about trust, about confidence. He taught us to enjoy the outdoors, taught us to love the music, but what he mostly taught was how to work hard, because this was the hardest-working guy. Three jobs. Social worker by day, adult educator by night, music teacher on weekends. He was a beautiful piano player...

I had a great relationship with him. I talked to him every day. When he passed it was a special time. I got on my bike...

Here Bill's tears started to fall.

I got on my bike and I rode to all the places, all the homes, all the schools and churches. I was left with everything. I was left with the greatest life that a son could have.

Bill stopped again and gulped several times and said, "Whew," as if surprised at how tough this was. I waited, and he didn't ask to stop the taping. We did take a commercial break though, and that gave him time to regroup.

So anyway (he said after the break), *the story was the day my dad died, I went on my bike and rode around to all the spots, to the house where he first lived with my mom, to the hospital where I was born, to the church where they were married, to Balboa Park, right next door here, where they had their wedding reception and where we would meet my dad every night after work because he was working two jobs.*

My mom would make the dinner, put it in the car, wrap it up in the blankets, we'd meet him in the park and we'd play, run, have so much fun, then he'd go off to work as a night-school teacher.

I read from a letter Bill's son wrote to Grandpa Ted, talking about what he had instilled in the hearts of his grandchildren. Bill listened and nodded and went on with his reminiscences.

Every day when I would leave my dad – because they lived in the same house for 54 years, the same house we all grew up in, and I lived 10 minutes away – every day I would say goodbye to him, or on the phone. He'd always say, "Thanks Bill, you're a wonderful son." And I'd look back at him and I'd say, "Dad, you got it wrong. I'm a lucky old son." And then we'd quickly start talking about music, because that was a line from a very famous song that one of his favorite musicians sang, Frankie Laine, and Jerry Garcia turned it into an absolute masterpiece of an anthem.

Roy:

The song is?

Walton:

"That Lucky Old Son."

As the interview ended and I was thanking Walton on camera, we had this exchange:

Walton:

You let me down.

Roy:

I did?

Walton:

You told me you weren't going to make me cry.

With Dennis Rodman

And all of his makeup is waterproof!

THE ALL-TEARS ALL-STARS

So now I've confessed that I made Rod Tidwell cry. I manipulated him, played him like a violin and wrung the tears out of him to give my TV show punch and drama.

But that was in a movie and I was parodying myself. Hey, if we can't parody ourselves, who can we parody?

In real life, believe it or not, I don't try to make people cry, and when they do weep during an interview it almost always takes me by surprise. Or do you think it was my game plan to get Bobby Knight to puddle up?

I am aware of my so-called reputation for having guests show their emotions. I once asked Mike Tyson if he has any regrets about his train wreck of a life and he sneered, "What do you want me to do, Roy, boo-hoo-hoo? Like everybody else on your show does? I got nothing to apologize for, I'm not gonna do a boo-hoo-hoo."

And Tyson didn't, but there you have it, the word is out: Roy's guests cry. Maybe one or two per year, but still.

In a minute I'll give you my For Cryin' Out Loud All-Star Team, the guys who have wept on my show. But first a word about the phenomenon.

If I do "make" people cry, to a much, much greater extent I "make" people laugh, think, reflect. For every athlete who has cried on my show there are hundreds who have laughed. But crying is more dramatic, so a handful of guests earn you a reputation, a reputation of which I am neither proud nor ashamed.

I do believe that what has nearly vanished from the so-called sports-interview landscape is honest emotion. There's a lot of yelling these days, a lot of quick/clever cutting repartee, guys in the hot seat, guys playing gotcha, shows with bells and buzzers, and the occasional in-depth four-minute "conversation."

I don't know whether there is a fear of real emotion, or if the pie-in-face style of personal interaction is simply what passes for cutting-edge. Call me old-school.

The first time an athlete cried on my show it took me by surprise. Almost every time it has happened since, it has taken me by surprise. I usually ask, gently, if the person would like to take a break, and that probably isn't something you'd ask if you were trying to exploit the guest's emotions. The "criers" almost never want to take a break. And I've never had a guest express embarrassment or regret for having shed a tear.

I don't try to milk the drama, but I don't shy away from sensitive or emotional topics. My "setup" of Tidwell in *Jerry Maguire* – "Your father leaves home on Christmas Eve..." – was a good send-up of myself, because I do try to give the audience background info, as in the following snippet from an interview with Kurt Warner: "Your story has been told many times, but bears repeating. The tragic loss – your wife losing both her parents in a tornado. Your adopted son essentially being blind. Even something mundane like being bitten by a spider before a tryout with the Chicago Bears..." As the saying goes, you can't make this stuff up.

After all these years, I'm not sure if a guest crying is great human theater or maudlin theatrics. But I do know this: As an interviewer, I am proudest when a soul is bared. Because while some critics mock me for my guests' tears, there are few places in sports television where the human heart is exposed.

That said, here are the guys who cried:

Dennis Rodman

He cried during several interviews, so Rodman is one guy whose tears seldom surprised me. He would cry while expressing regret over his bad behavior, then he'd go out and behave badly again. I felt kind of like his priest.

On one show Rodman must have cried 15 times in 20 minutes. He was talking about his daughter and how he wasn't allowed to see her. I said, "Wait a minute, your wife is preventing you from seeing your daughter?" He said, "Well, no, she lets me visit." I said, "So it's not exactly that you can't see your daughter." At that, he cried some more.

I won't say Rodman's tears were fake, but they were theatrical. On that program his hair was dyed green, he wore dark glasses, and the tears flowed down from under his shades.

After my show, Rodman did *Oprah* and other national shows, so I guess my program was the first stop on his Tears Over America tour.

Mike Garrett

Mike was the first to cry on my program. It was about 1980, not long after the end of Garrett's outstanding pro career, and the subject turned to his rookie year with the Kansas City Chiefs.

Garrett talked about how in a team meeting an assistant coach scolded him, "If you don't run the trap play better than that, you're going to wind up working as a day laborer like your dad."

As Garrett told the story, the tears spilled. He talked about how his father, a common laborer, worked heroically to raise four kids, and how it didn't bother Mike if a coach berated him, but do not ever mock his father.

Over the years that has been a common theme – tears for a mother or father for whom the athlete can never properly express his love, gratitude and respect.

Barry Bonds

I usually assume a guest's tears are genuine. With Barry, I was never sure. I'm not suggesting Bonds was acting when he talked and cried about his late grandfather, the promises Barry made to him as he was dying, and of not having properly said goodbye to his grandfather.

All I'm saying is that with Barry, everything is different. I can't question the depth of his feelings. All I know is that his crying felt a bit soap-operaish.

Bobby Knight

I asked Knight about when he was paying tribute to his senior players in an annual ceremony at Indiana's Assembly Hall, and he introduced his son Patrick as his all-time favorite player.

Instantly, the emotion from that moment came back to Knight, and if tears didn't spill, his eyes certainly were close to overflow. He talked about how he had been a tough father, sometimes unpleasant, and how hard it must be to be Bobby Knight's kid. This is a son who caused Knight some anguish, got busted for a DUI and Bobby kicked him off the team.

Knight, like Bonds, exists in a different emotional world from most of the rest of us, but until that moment I had never seen Knight tear up.

Jerry Rice

Nobody's more emotional than Jerry, who might be the toughest man ever to stride a football field. Catch balls over the middle and laugh at the danger, shrug off the vicious hits? No problem. Talk about having to retire from the game you love? Problem. Tears.

In one of our interviews Jerry cried about crying. We were talking about the time he was injured and TV cameras caught him crying in frustration on the sidelines. Recalling that moment, Rice cried.

Jimmy Johnson

He cried when talking about being fired by the Cowboys. "All I ever tried to do my whole life was please my daddy," Jimmy said. "And my daddy's so proud of me being coach of the Cowboys, and I said, 'Daddy, I will no longer be coach of the Dallas Cowboys.'"

Barry Switzer

Funny, but Johnson's successor as Cowboys coach was also a crier, also when talking about his daddy. Switzer's father was a moonshiner, gambler, spent most of his life on either the wrong side of the law or on the fringes. But Barry loved his daddy and teared up while defending him as a man of honor.

Switzer is also the only guest, so far, who threatened to punch me. It was when I asked him about his Oklahoma coaching days, when his teams were known for their outlaw antics.

"Anyone ever threaten to punch you in the mouth?" Switzer asked me. "We'll I'm gonna be the first."

(Boxer Buster Douglas seemed ready to take a poke at me when I asked him about the widespread perception that he tanked matches. Fortunately, the interview took place in the middle of a ring, the day before one of his fights, and Buster seldom hurt anybody in the ring.)

Sugar Ray Leonard

A charming guy, always at ease with the public and media, but he usually avoided digging beneath the surface and revealing much. But in one of our interviews following his retirement, after his problems with cocaine and marital infidelity had become known, I asked him about his son, Little Ray, who was born just before Leonard won an Olympics gold medal in '76. I asked Ray what it had been like for his son to live on the roller-coaster of his father's life.

"I'll tell you a story," Sugar Ray said. "My son decided to write me a poem, he called it 'The Gift.'"

Ray took an old piece of paper from his pocket and read the poem about how a child is a gift, and even after hard times and turmoil, father and son are still precious to one another. Sugar Ray was crying and couldn't finish the poem, but he did talk about his regrets of having let his son down, how Sugar Ray tarnished the gift that was his son. It was a side of Ray I'd never seen.

Michael Irvin

He cried twice. Once when he talked of being at his dying father's bedside, promising he would never let his father down, but drugs and alcohol caused him to break that promise.

The second cry was when Irvin talked about the hit that ended his career, left him temporarily paralyzed on the field, realizing he would never play ball with his son again. Irvin is no candidate for sainthood, but he has copped to his mistakes, and his emotion in those two interview moments was very real and human.

George Brett

Everybody loves George Brett, he's the ultimate guy's guy. George and his brothers Ken and Bobby were California beach kids, but their dad Jack was a tough guy from New York, a Marine who stormed the beach at Normandy, and a very demanding father.

George hit .390 in 1980 and that winter his father phoned him several times to berate him for not being tough enough to hit the five more hits to get to .400.

George talked about how years later his father, dying of cancer, phoned him and said, "I've never been much of a father, but I feel like a king because of what you and your brothers gave me. Not just because you were great ballplayers, but because you're great guys."

As George told the story, he teared up and said, "I really can't do this, it's too hard, let's go to something else."

But before we moved on, George said, "I really never made peace with my father, I was never able to let go of how hard we were on each other. He'd grind me and I'd fire back… It's just hard, because you don't have a second chance."

Emmitt Smith

In my book, Emmitt is one of the great character guys. He was never a sensational interview, but one day he talked about his grandmother. Emmitt grew up in Pensacola, his family was dirt poor. His grandmother Essie was a paraplegic, and for much of Emmitt's youth, age 11 to 15, he and Essie took care of one another.

She raised him and Emmitt bathed her, took her to the bathroom, fed her. I was unaware of this story until he brought it up.

"When people talk about sacrifice," Smith said, "they don't realize what real sacrifice is. I think about my grandma, how much she never got to do because she couldn't walk, how she never got to see me play a single football game, and I was the pride and joy of her life."

I could see Emmitt starting to go, but he went on.

"I just feel sad for her, that she never got to see me run because she couldn't walk. I learned so much about what it is to be a man just by watching her endure, seeing her pride."

Magic Johnson

My admiration for Magic is huge and I love having him on the show because he never holds back

He has cried twice. Once when talking about his father working three jobs and sacrificing for the family, Magic and his nine brothers and sisters.

The second cry was when Magic talked about his post-basketball career of providing economic opportunities for thousands of people in the inner city.

"I'm crying tears of joy," Magic said, "because my life has mattered to other people, my involvement in the community has mattered, and that's the greatest dream I could ever have."

Greg Louganis

Maybe the greatest Olympic diver ever, Greg was diagnosed with the HIV virus the year after Magic Johnson was diagnosed. I asked Louganis what worries him.

"I worry every day that I live alone and that I'll die alone," Louganis said, as the tears fell. "You have no idea what it feels like to know you'll be alone and abandoned, that when you're in a hospital bed dying of AIDS, nobody will want to be there for you. I don't want to live alone or die alone." Whew.

Rick Majerus

His father died of a massive heart attack when Rick was young, and the emotion of that tragedy came rushing back to Majerus when, as a coach at Utah, he had to call Keith Van Horne into his office and tell Keith that his father had died. Telling the story, Rick cried.

Lyle Alzado

He was thin and sick and wasting away; it was the last interview Alzado ever did. Several people who knew him well tell me they believe Alzado died of AIDS contracted from growth hormone extracted from infected cadavers in a clinic in Mexico.

Lyle did the interview because his dying mission was to warn the public, kids mostly, of the dangers and stupidity of using performance-enhancing drugs.

Alzado's tears were of regret and shame, and maybe the frustration of knowing his advice would be widely ignored.

Wes Unseld

He wept while telling a very simple and beautiful story about how the greatest lesson his father ever taught him was to love his mother.

Hubie Brown and Bill Walton

They both cried when sharing memories of their fathers. When I look at the tapes of those interviews, I get emotional.

But one person who has never cried on the show is yours truly. I get caught up in the emotion, sure, but when a guest gets to the point where tears are flowing, I try to step back figuratively and take myself out of the picture.

Howard Cosell, for all his journalistic greatness, was shameless when interjecting himself into an emotional interview. "I spoke to Darrell Porter about his tragic drug addiction," Howard would say, "and I exclusively learned that his road has been a long and painful one."

At the point of tears, my guest doesn't need my guidance or sympathy. Ideally, they forget I'm even there and that they are on TV, and they simply express themselves.

The closest I ever came to tears? That would be the time a guest turned the tables on me, put me in the spotlight.

It was 1992, in Los Angeles, and the city was in the turmoil of the so-called Rodney King riots. My two guests were former Negro League baseball players Sammie Haynes and Ray Welmaker, promoting an organization that assists destitute former Negro Leaguers.

We talked about baseball, and hard times, and near the end of the interview Haynes said, "I got something to give you, Roy Firestone."

Haynes, who had been blind for more than 25 years, unfastened a pin from his lapel.

"I been listening to this show for many years," Haynes said, "and I realize it don't matter to you about color, it only matters the heart. I'm gonna take this pin off and put it on your lapel, because there's nothing more important in life than getting past all the differences that we have, and remembering that we're all just people."

Sammie thanked me for all the times over the years that the show dealt with racism and race issues. He handed me the pin and said, "Tell me what this say, Roy."

The pin had five tiny blocks of color-white, black, red, yellow and brown-and a heart in the middle. But no words.

"What it *say* there, Roy," Sammie said, "is all the colors have to be together. In the middle it say, 'It takes love.'"

Here was a guy who had every reason to be angry and bitter, and he was talking about love.

I thanked him and went quickly to a commercial break.

What did you want me to do? Stay there and boo-hoo-hoo?

With Steffi Graf and Andre Agassi

Beyond tennis, two true champions.

chapter

5

THE GIANT

Question from the audience:

"Which athlete do you most admire?"

Lance Armstrong:

"Andre Agassi, absolutely. Its not even close."

As it became obvious that the cause was lost, that the old guy was going to lose, it was almost as if the 23,000 fans in the stadium were watching a bullfight and cheering for the bull.

Andre Agassi was dragging himself around the court in obvious pain. For the third day in a row he had taken an injection in his spine just to allow him to limp onto the court to compete in a tournament he knew he could not win.

It was the third round of the 2006 U.S. Open and Agassi was saying goodbye.

Having survived an incredible five-set, four-hour match two days earlier, Agassi was toast. Nothing left in the tank. He was losing to the unknown Benny Becker, who, with a matador flourish, finished off Agassi with an ace down the middle. Andre, whose finest tennis weapon was his return of serve, was ushered out with an ace.

Agassi sank into his courtside chair, covered his head with a towel and sobbed.

Then he composed himself, rose, gave his signature four-corners bow to the packed house, walked to a microphone and addressed the fans.

"The scoreboard said I lost today," Agassi said, tears in his eyes, "but what the scoreboard doesn't say is what I have found. And over the last 21 years I have found loyalty. You have pulled for me on the court, and also in life. I've found inspiration. You have willed me to succeed even in my lowest moments. And I've found generosity. You have given me your shoulders to stand on to reach for my dreams – dreams I could never have reached without you. Over the last 21 years I have found you and I will take you, and the memory of you, with me for the rest of my life. Thank you."

Then Andre limped out of the stadium, one of the most compelling and beloved figures in American sports. And a man who took us all by surprise.

Nobody saw Andre Agassi coming. Not *this* Andre Agassi.

Back when Agassi was a teen phenom laying waste to the dignity of tennis, all we saw coming was trouble. A headache with long blond hair.

Remember that Andre Agassi? Spat at chair umpires... threw tantrums... acted like the spoiled, vaguely troubled kid that he was. If John McEnroe was Superbrat, Agassi was Superpunk – all bad attitude, misdirected talent and maybe a glimmer of charm under the smugness.

Who would have predicted back then that Agassi would become the poster dude for tennis, for hard work and dedication, for competitive grit... and for caring?

Relatively late in his career Andre re-invented himself, took his game and his tennis legacy to a higher level, with hard work.

"I believe a lot in momentum," Andre told me during one of our interviews. "If you can stay disciplined long enough, it then becomes a way of life, and then things start happening."

Like Grand Slam wins, eight in all.

Even more startling, who would have predicted that the angry kid not only would avoid some major social catastrophe, but would channel his fame and energy and heart into helping disadvantaged kids, that his compassion would become his calling card, even more so than his legendary, gritty-yet-pretty game?

It's a little hard for me to talk about Agassi without waxing sappy. The generosity of his spirit blows me away. All you have to do to appreciate Agassi is to see him in two places:

One, backstage at his annual fundraising celebrity concert in Las Vegas. Somehow Agassi lures almost every big star in show biz to this event, and it's incredible to see the energy and enthusiasm that radiates from the host to his guests.

Elton John was at one of the galas and he told me, "When I was a drug addict and an alcoholic, my mother used to say, 'I don't want any gifts, but I want a piece of your time.' That's the most valuable thing you can give, and that's what Andre has done for the kids."

Two, you have to see Andre on the back streets of Las Vegas, in the city's ghetto, where Agassi has brought hope to thousands of disadvantaged youngsters, building or helping build a recreation center, a charter school, and a facility for battered children.

"How do you take kids who have no opportunity," Agassi asked me, "who have no reason to get up in the morning, how do you give them a chance? How do you give them something to be excited about? If you want it bad enough, you can do it. Life is a gift and everybody deserves a shot at it. To live without dreams and without hope, it would be like prison."

I asked Agassi how he finds the energy for his three lives: tennis, his family, and his charity work.

"For me, resting doesn't get it done," he said. "There will come a day for me to rest, but it won't be on this earth. As far as I'm concerned, this is about being all that you can be, in many areas of life. The hub of my wheel is who I am, and tennis is just one of the spokes.

"What gets it up for me is the challenge, asking more of yourself, ending the day saying, 'I might not believe, I might have my doubts, but one thing I know is, I'm always going to try, I'm going to fight.'"

He took his fight to the back streets of his home town, far from the city's neon lights. I'd like to share with you a story written by a friend of mine, Scott Ostler, who visited Agassi's legacy.

A PLACE TO HEAL

by Scott Ostler

In this city built on wild dreams, there is a corner reserved for the worst nightmares. If you want to see what it's like to be dealt a bad hand, to have the dice go stone cold, come with me to Child Haven. It's a county facility, but much of the money to build it and run it comes from charitable donations.

In the eight cottages of this little village, children from newborns to teenagers receive better attention and care than guests at a five-star hotel, and Lord, do they need it. The kids here can tell you horror stories, and the ones too young to talk tell the stories with their eyes and with their scars.

In the brand-new Andre Agassi Cottage for Fragile Children, for kids with extreme medical needs, you meet Cheryl. She has beautiful brown skin, except the spots on both hands and forearms that are several shades lighter from having been dipped in scalding water, and except for the several cigarette burns on her body.

When Cheryl was admitted, she recoiled in horror from every man, including Leon Ireland, the Senior Child Development Specialist. Cheryl clung desperately to a female attendant, never taking her eyes off Leon while whimpering, "Is he going to burn me?"

Leon has been here 28 years and he has seen a lot, but that got to him. That brought the big man close to tears.

About 3,100 children are admitted to Child Haven each year. They arrive burned and broken, abused and abandoned, sick and scared, hurting from the tips of their fingers to the depth of their souls. They stay here for a day or a year, long enough to catch a break and to experience what for many of them is their first dose of the miracle drug love. This is a repair shop for children's souls.

Business is brisk. The center's hotline receives 800 calls per month. On one recent eight-hour shift, the campus admitted 30 children.

School-age kids at Child Haven attend the Agassi Center for Education. ACE, get it? Agassi objected to putting his name on the buildings he and his charity helped fund, but people who know such things argued that his name would help in fundraising. Andre is a local legend and if he's in, a lot of high-rollers want a piece of the action.

Before Agassi Foundation money arrived, the Child Haven school was one small room in a dilapidated building. Now the 140-or-so school-age children have a beautiful brick building with six schoolrooms equipped with computers, books and a smiling, first-rate teacher. It's a real school. Most of the kids who come here have been shorted, education-wise, so this is about serious catch-up.

One schoolroom is home to dozens of live animals – snakes, lizards, birds. The guinea pig, named Andre, was brought here to heal after being abused by a family dog.

When a visitor tours the cottage for grammar school-aged girls, they all stand. Each young woman looks the visitor in the eye, shakes his hand firmly, gives her name and asks politely, "What's yours?"

"Some people (outside) think this place is bad," says Barbara, who is 14 and in her fourth stay at Child Haven. "We're not in here for being bad, we're in here to be protected. Some of the girls don't want to leave here. The people here talk to us about our feelings and our problems. They're like the mothers and fathers we want."

Back in the Fragile Care Cottage, Leon Ireland remembers what it was like not long ago, before the new building. Critical-care kids were jammed into corners of other buildings, reinforcing their life view that they just don't fit in. Leon surveys the beautiful facility and says quietly, "This is what you call a miracle."

Miracles are the specialty of the house. When a three-month-old baby was brought in, blind and deaf from being shaken, Ireland refused to acknowledge the diagnosis and gradually discovered that the child could see and hear. Leon is a hard man to discourage.

Leon and two-year-old burn victim Cheryl now get along famously. Soon she will be released to a new home. She will be remembered at Child Haven for her giggle, her intelligence, her courage and her mastery of the "Hokey Pokey."

Now she climbs onto Leon's lap and tells him, "I love you." Cheryl finally wore the big man down. She convinced Leon that she's not such a bad kid after all.

When Agassi's final moment on the stage was over, when he'd been aced off the court at the '06 U.S. Open, he flopped into his courtside chair, wrapped a towel around his head and sobbed.

The fans stood and cheered. The passion and commitment Andre brought to his two decades in the public eye came flooding back to him. Life is an echo; you get back what you send out, and what Agassi was getting back was love.

After his farewell address Andre limped off the court and into the locker room, nearly sick with pain and fatigue, tears still rolling down his cheeks. When he entered, the other players did something unheard of – they stood and applauded.

It was a great way to go out, except Agassi wasn't really going out. His tennis was over, but his battle will never end. Unlike many great athletes, whose legacy is what they accomplished on the field or court, Agassi's ultimate legacy will transcend tennis.

His legacy will be the school, the critical-care facility, the gymnasium and tennis courts he has built for the disadvantaged kids of his home town, and his ongoing efforts to keep those facilities pumping out the love.

In one of our interviews I asked Andre if there is one aspect of his game that represents him as a human being.

"It's the return of service, Roy," Agassi said. "When something is hit my way, I always try to return it. I may not have the strongest serve, but I'm a guy who finds a way to return service."

Over the years, as the spoiled brat evolved into a man, Andre came to realize how many people contributed to his glory, how many provided him with priceless service, how many simply gave him love.

Sometimes it's funny how an athlete's sports character can reflect his human character. Magic Johnson is a superstar because he handed out assists, on the court and in the community.

For Andre Agassi, his legacy will forever be his return of service.

Dikembe Mutombo

Lifting up a nation.

chapter

6

A TRUE WARRIOR

The athlete I admire most?

When I was a kid, that would have been an easy call. I admired 'em all, unconditionally. I assumed that their athletic greatness carried over to their character, that all great athletes were also great people.

I wouldn't say I became cynical or jaded, because I find admirable qualities in so many of the athletes I meet, and I've met hundreds. But I learned long ago that all superstars aren't superstar people.

It seems that we stretch to create super people out of super athletes. We sanitize their lives, play up the good stuff, build them into storybook characters. We in the media sometimes look the other way on negative stuff, maybe in a subconscious effort to maintain our access to the players.

More and more I realize that in order to become great at what they do, athletes have to be selfish, or at least self-centered. Their world view can shrink to the size of the court or field on which they play, or the size of the estate they show off on MTV's *Cribs*.

But once in a great while I encounter an athlete who makes me look up and say, "Wow, *that's* a human being."

That's Dikembe Mutombo.

I have met many generous and big-hearted athletes who give to charity, help fight a disease, aid a worthy cause, even try to save a neighborhood.

But Dikembe Mutombo is trying to save an entire *country*. Which is absolutely impossible and insane, but he doesn't care, and his work and his money are making a huge impact. When I die, I just hope I'm not standing in the line at the Pearly Gates behind Dikembe Mutombo, because that would be one tough act to follow.

Every time I interview Dikembe, I ask him to say his full name. In his deep rich voice he says it proudly: "Dikembe Mutombo Mpolondo Mukamba Jean Jacques Wamutombo." At least part of his name means "warrior."

You have to be an NBA fan to know Mutombo is a veteran backup center for the Houston Rockets. Although he has been an All-Star eight times in his 15-year career, he has never been a glamour-type player. He's a defender and shot-blocker, does the dirty work, the heavy lifting. He was voted the NBA's Defensive Player of the Year four times.

If you collect bubblegum cards, you would have to trade about a dozen Mutombos to get one Shaq or one Steve Nash. But on my all-character team, I wouldn't trade Mutombo for 10 superstars. He's a superstar in life, right up there with the late Arthur Ashe on my scale.

Let me tell you about this guy.

Dikembe is huge... 7-foot-2 and 260 pounds. He wears size 23 shoes and is fluent in nine languages. He is from Kinshasa, the capital of the Democratic Republic of the Congo, formerly Zaire. Zaire was famous as the country that hosted the first Ali-Frazier fight, "The Rumble in the Jungle." That jungle is still rumbling, unfortunately, with civil war and rampant disease.

Even in urban Kinshasa, health care is all but nonexistent. More than a million people each year die from diseases that could be easily prevented and cured, if enough people cared.

Do you worry about your child or loved one dying of malaria, measles or polio? You could drop a nuclear bomb every day in the

Congo and not do the human damage that these "conquered" diseases are doing. AIDS is a serial killer, too, for kids and adults.

The Congo is one-fourth the size of the United States, with a population of 50 million, and roughly zero of those people are free from the terror of disease and lack of medical care. You talk about terrorism, *that's* real terrorism.

Dikembe's father was a worker, considered well-paid because he made $34 per month. Dikembe was the seventh of 10 children, and several other relatives lived with the family in their home, 19 people in four rooms.

So he was raised in semi-poverty and full squalor, in a city and a country where death due to ordinary disease is common, and where civil war has raged for as long as anyone can remember.

After high school, Dikembe was offered a USAID scholarship to Georgetown, where he intended to study medicine, become a doctor and return to the Congo. But he took a detour. Invited to try out for the basketball team by coach John Thompson, Mutombo became a star. He did pretty well in basketball, too.

Dikembe didn't speak a word of English when he arrived in America. He told me he was amazed at how many of his fellow students treated their educational opportunity so casually. That lukewarm approach to education was more foreign to Dikembe than any other aspect of America. He graduated in four years with dual degrees in linguistics and diplomacy.

Then he became an NBA star, a defensive superstar whose signature is waggling his right index finger scoldingly at a player whose shot he had just blocked.

Dikembe became wealthy beyond his dreams. Kinshasa and the poverty and disease of the Congo, that was all behind him, right? Isn't that the dream, to make it big and put the hard life behind you? Sure, you send some money back home to help the folks, buy mom a house, buy clothes for the family. But you settle into your new life, your new country, your wealth and celebrity... and health.

Think about it. What was Dikembe going to do? Save the Congo by himself? That is too absurd to even consider, unless you are Dikembe Mutombo.

He has poured money, energy and heart into an ongoing effort to stamp out misery and illness in his native country. I am amazed at the two worlds this man straddles – the NBA, with its wealth and privilege, private planes and locker rooms more lavish than four-star hotels; and the Congo, with despair and hopelessness that must seem as deep as the pits of Hell, especially after you've lived on the other side.

In the off season, Dikembe travels to Africa to hold basketball clinics and assist in humanitarian work. In 1999 his efforts helped 8.2 *million* children under the age of five receive polio vaccine, some of which he administered himself, dropping the medicine onto the tongues of kids who otherwise would have suffered and died.

He has established his own foundation. Among his donations: $5,000 to repair the leaky roof of the Congo embassy building in Washington D.C. He bankrolled his country's women's basketball team in the '96 Olympics and personally helped train the men's and women's teams, and helped finance the track-and-field team. In a Congo ghetto, he rebuilt a squalid dorm for poor orphans into a sparkling school for the needy kids.

And then Dikembe set about to build a hospital. Not a hospital room. Not a hospital wing. A hospital. The project was started in 1997 and the hospital opened in Februrary 2007.

In the Congo there hasn't been a new hospital built in 40 years. Disease and civil war have ravaged the country for decades, draining what finances might have been available for health care.

But a new 300-bed hospital has been constructed, bankrolled by Mutumbo. The old hospital in Kinshasa has one outdated X-ray machine, which is probably powered by rats on a treadmill. There are only three ambulances in the city, and here is where the story gets very personal for Mutombo.

In 1998 Dikembe's mother, Biamba Marie Mutombo, suffered a stroke, or at least that's the best guess. There was no ambulance service available because of the shortage and because the rebels were threatening to kill anybody who was on the streets. Biamba Mutombo died while waiting for an ambulance that never came, to take her to a hospital that wouldn't have had the room or facilities to treat her.

So Dikembe resolved to build a hospital, at a cost of about $29 million. So far he has kicked in about $15 million of his own money and panhandled for the rest.

Mutombo deputized himself as his own No. 1 fund-raiser. He has approached virtually every NBA player with his hand out. He asks for $10,000, says that if each player gave $10,000 – which, by the way, is an afternoon shopping spree for most of these guys – they would wipe out more human suffering than they could ever imagine.

As Steve Rushin wrote in *Sports Illustrated*, "In professional sports, putting your money where you mouth is usually means getting gold teeth, but Mutombo has received hundreds of thousands of dollars from Patrick Ewing, Juwon Howard, Tracy McGrady, Alonzo Mouring and Yao Ming, among many others."

Dikembe tells me that when he sees the avarice and the greed and excessive lifestyle of some NBA players, it makes him almost physically ill. But he doesn't let that get him down. He finds positive in everyone.

This man has a spirit that lights up a room. Dikembe is always upbeat, even jovial, a great person to talk to, to be around. He refuses to let what he has seen, and the insurmountable battle ahead, dull his senses or sour him. He seems supercharged by the challenge, and he enjoys life, whether he's kicking back in the luxury of NBA life, or wading armpit-deep in squalor in the darkest ghettos of a country that civilization has turned its back on.

For Dikembe, charity work isn't a photo-op. It's not a United Way commercial or a fund-raiser golf tournament. It's a lifetime of hard work and sacrifice. When he talks of his work, he exudes a passion and sense of urgency unlike that of any athlete I've ever been around.

His giving never stops. He and wife Rose are raising seven children, four of whom are Dikembe's nieces and nephews that the Mutombos have adopted.

It's almost unbelievable, isn't it, the capacity of one person's heart?

With Albert Belle, Hank Aaron, and Barry Bonds

Luckily, they're letting Hank do the talking.

THIS ALBERT IS NO PRINCE

My most dangerous interview?

Reggie Jackson can be difficult, challenging, confrontational, condescending, even hostile. But there always seemed to be humanity behind the bluster, something to keep you amused or intrigued.

Eddie Murray wasn't much fun one-on-one. Bobby Knight almost cost me my job, so he's on my dangerous list.

But Albert Belle gets the nod. He provided me with my only near-death experience as an interviewer.

Let me set this up with a story from Albert Belle's college career.

I got this from Skip Bertman, who was my high school history and driver's ed teacher, and the school's baseball coach. He's a terrific guy, wonderful teacher, and he had a great positive influence on me back then. If you can't get along with Skip Bertman, you can't get along with Winnie the Pooh.

Skip became baseball coach at Louisiana State University, where his teams would win the College World Series five times. In 1987 one of Bertman's star players was Albert Belle, who back then went by his nickname, Joey (his middle name is Jojuan). LSU was playing in the Southeastern Conference tournament, and Skip had a problem with Joey not hustling.

Belle didn't jog out grounders, he *sauntered* 'em out.

Skip warned Joey: Hustle or get benched. Joey just glowered.

One game during the conference tournament, Joey went into the stands after a fan who hurled racist taunts at him. Then, the last straw: Belle hit a ball off the outfield fence and walked to first base.

So Skip suspended Belle for the College World Series.

Next morning Skip answered the phone in his office. It was Joey's mother, who happened to be a schoolteacher, as was Joey's dad.

The conversation went something like this:

"How are you, Mrs. Belle?"

"Well, I'm a little upset. I understand that Joseph is not going to be playing in the championship series."

"That's correct."

"Is there a reason for this?"

"I told Joey he would be benched if he didn't hustle, and he didn't hustle."

"Is there anything I can do about this?"

"No, it really has nothing to do with you, Mrs. Belle. Joey was warned, he didn't run out a hit, and now he's suspended."

"I see. Well, I just want you to know, coach, that I can't be responsible for whatever may happen to you."

"Are you threatening me, Mrs. Belle?"

"I can't be responsible. I'll just leave it at that."

Now we fast forward to 1995. Belle, who now goes by his real first name Albert, leads the Cleveland Indians into the World Series. Before a Series game, Belle chases NBC reporter Hannah Storm out of the dugout with a vile verbal tirade.

Later that month, after Halloween trick-or-treaters egg his condo, Belle chases them in his Jeep and bumps one of the guys with his bumper.

I tried to set up an interview with Belle. Some would wonder why I would want to interview such a despicable character. Good question. By now, Belle's list of serious "incidents" is long and ugly. Many in baseball have written him off as a bad guy.

However, if I only go after "good guys" to interview, my career would be pretty limited, and I would miss a lot of interesting people.

Besides, absolute value judgments are risky. I'm not going to tell you that under all that anger and bullying, Belle is a puppy dog. But as a kid, he was an Eagle Scout. He could spell backwards at age three. While in college, he worked as a substitute teacher. He quietly donates large sums to scholarship funds and to youth baseball clinics. He has written newspaper columns – in one instance, a poem to fans.

Also, Belle was in the middle of a Hall of Fame caliber career. An interesting, if flawed, character. A tough interview, but I hate to duck a challenge. I had "interviewed" Belle a couple years earlier, sort of. He refused to talk to me, so I got Barry Bonds to interview him for me, as a joke.

Now it's time for spring training in '96, and I get a phone call from John Hart, the general manager of the Cleveland Indians, Belle's team.

"I know you've been trying to get an interview with Albert," Hart says, "and I know you haven't had much luck. We're really going to try to make Albert more fan-friendly, for his benefit and for ours, and we think you're the guy who could sit down with him and show that he's got some good qualities that people haven't really seen."

"You really think he's got a nice side?" I asked.

"I think so, and I think you're the guy to expose it."

"I'll be glad to sit down with him," I say. "When and where?"

We set it up for the first week of spring training, in Winter Haven. I set it up through the Indians' PR person, Bobby DiBiasi, a nice and very competent fellow.

Bob tells me, "Everybody in the organization is eager for you to interview Albert, because this really is his last shot. Bring your camera crew, you can follow him around, show him signing autographs, that kind of thing."

I fly to Florida with my crew, at a cost of about $10,000.

Day one: I walked into the clubhouse. Albert is at his locker, playing music on his stereo, very loudly, and no one dares ask him to turn it down. He's swinging a bat. I walk up and put out my hand. He looks at my hand as though unfamiliar with the concept of the handshake. He continues to stare at my hand as if it's a projection coming out of the middle of my stomach.

We're not really bonding here. I slowly reel my hand back in and walk away. I find Bobby and tell him what happened.

"He's just feeling you out, Roy," Bobby said. "It won't be a problem."

A little later in the morning, I approach Belle standing near the batting cage.

"I know you've got work to do, Albert," I say, "I just want to let you know we're here to interview you this weekend."

He looks at me like I'm speaking Martian.

"What? I don't know what you're talking about. I got nothing to say to you or any-bleeping-body else. Just get out of my bleeping face."

I go back to Bobby.

"Albert is Albert," Bobby says. "I'm sure you've dealt with people like this. It'll be cool."

My camera crew follows Albert around for three days, gets some footage of him signing autographs, visiting Ted Williams and Ted's museum. I would find out later that Belle caused a stir at the Williams gig, first refusing to get into the limo to the event, then refusing to get out.

Now it's Saturday, the designated day for the interview. A story in today's paper says that Major League Baseball has fined

Belle $50,000 for his tirade against Hannah Storm, so I check with Bobby.

"You think we'll have any problem today?

"No, in fact this is the perfect day to talk to him, because I think he wants to put this stuff behind him, kind of get a fresh start, let people know what he's really like."

Bobby leaves and I'm killing time in his office and a paper comes over the fax machine. It's a cover letter from Terry Belle, Albert's fraternal twin brother. It's addressed to Bobby, it says, "Bobby, here's my draft of the statement Albert will read."

The next page is the apology to Hannah Storm that Albert is to read at a press conference. He doesn't even write his own apology! Unbelievable. The only way this apology could be less sincere would be if Belle gives a batboy $20 to read it for him.

(Belle once read an apology for another incident, then stuffed the paper in his back pocket and theatrically rolled his eyes. When you look up "contrition" in the dictionary, Albert's picture ain't there.)

Now it's 4:30 and we're supposed to do the interview at 5:00, so my crew and I can fly home. I'm sensing that this might not be the best day to talk to Belle, but we set this thing up weeks ago, and he has known about it for several days.

I walk into the clubhouse and approach Belle.

"Albert, I wonder if you would be kind enough to sit down with us and do this interview we've set up."

He glares at me like he wants to kill me and is extra mad because he can't decide on the best method. It's a little frightening. One of his own teammates nicknamed Belle "Snapper."

"Get the bleep out of my face!" he snaps.

He picks up a bat and repeats his message. "Get out of my face! All of you stink!"

The clubhouse is deserted except for Albert, me and a trainer. As Belle starts ranting, Sandy Alomar walks in from the shower, wearing shower shoes and a towel. Alomar sees Belle flipping out and says to me, "What's going on here, Roy?"

I know Sandy pretty well, he's one of the sweetest people in the world.

"We're having a little issue," I say to Sandy.

Albert cuts me off and says to Sandy, "It's none of your bleeping business!"

Alomar is a big guy, about 6' 3", solid, almost as big as Belle. And not a wimp.

Alomar goes, "Excuse me?"

"It's none of your bleeping business," Belle says. "Get the bleep out of my business!"

Sandy looks at me and says, "Is he giving you a problem?"

"Actually, Sandy, it's just that we have a disagreement."

"There's no bleeping disagreement," Belle says. "I'm not doing your bleeping interview. You can kiss my ass."

Now Sandy is getting agitated. He says, "Albert, you can't talk to him that way. That's not the right way to talk to someone."

"You want a piece of me?" Belle asks.

"A piece of your what?" Alomar says. "I'll kick your ass, and I'll kick anyone else's ass you want to bring in here."

It's crazy. Belle is in his full uniform, Alomar is still dripping wet from the shower. It's like a bad gladiator movie. What am I going to do if they go at it? Try to stop two of baseball's biggest stars from battling to the death over Belle's refusal to do an interview?

The yelling and screaming gets wilder, and the trainer steps between Belle and Alomar to try to keep the peace. Just then, manager Mike Hargrove pops out of his office. He can see we've got trouble.

"Roy," Hargrove says, pulling me aside, "you're going to have to go. I know John and Bobby set this interview up, but I don't know what this guy might do."

Now Belle has a bat and he's swinging at chairs, completely crazed, re-arranging the clubhouse furniture. After several healthy swings and broken chairs, Albert storms out of the clubhouse, still in his uniform, gets in his car and drives away.

I don't get the interview, but I do live to tell about it.

Postscript

Maybe I just caught Albert at a bad time.

A few years later I run into him in at the ESPN restaurant in Baltimore. Belle had just been traded to the Orioles and I'm a lifelong Orioles fan (and their former spring-training batboy). So I'm thinking I'll say hi, wish him well with his new team, put that crazy '96 incident behind us.

Albert is sitting with his brother, who couldn't be more pleasant. I chat for a minute, then turn to Albert, put out my hand, wish him luck. He does not glance up from his pizza.

Albert and I have decided not to be friends.

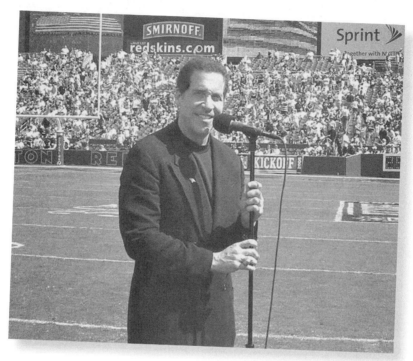

At FedEx Field, September 11, 2005

Do I look relaxed? I'm terrified.

chapter
8

HELP!
IS IT "STREAMING" OR "GLEAMING"?

Let me give you some life advice. Be kind to children, give generously to charity, and, next time you go to a ballgame, cut the National Anthem singer some slack.

When Francis Scott Key was inspired to write "The Star Spangled Banner," I wonder if he knew how much anxiety he was inspiring in future generations of ballpark anthem singers, including yours truly.

It's a tough song to sing. Beautiful and rousing, but tough. Robert Klein says it's a song written for a goose. No matter where you start "Oooo say," no matter how low you begin, eventually you wind up honking like a goose.

At the ballpark, you add the huge, fired-up crowd, the crazy ballpark acoustics and the assorted emotional baggage, and the degree of difficulty is squared and cubed.

I'm not new to this gig. The Florida Marlins asked me to sing the National Anthem before the first game of the franchise's history, in 1994. I'm from Florida, graduated from the University of Miami and worked in the city, so the terror factor was mitigated by my home-field advantage. All my friends and family were in the house that night, waiting for me to blow it, but they would have forgiven me. I survived, even though my microphone wasn't open for the first three bars.

The Dodgers had me sing the Anthem before a playoff game in 1995, and that's pressure.

But those moments barely register on the terror meter compared to singing the National Anthem before the Redskins-Bears game on September 11th, 2005, the NFL season opener at FedEx Field, home of the Washington Redskins.

That, my friends, was pressure.

Joe Gibbs was the Redskins coach, a great guy, by the way, and a few months earlier I performed at a Joe Gibbs Foundation fundraiser for underprivileged children. Redskins' owner Daniel Snyder was there and apparently enjoyed the show.

So I get a phone call from the Redskins front office, a man asking if I'd he interested in singing the National Anthem before a game. I said, sure. I'd love to, any time.

A few weeks went by, I didn't hear anything. Then the team rep called again and asked if I would do it. They would fly me and a guest to DC. I said, "Absolutely, when would you like me to do it?"

"The first game, September 11," he said, "It's a nationally televised game. We're having a special ceremony in honor of Sept 11th, we'll have a giant American flag on the field, a military-jet flyover, and also on the field we'll have families who lost loved ones in the attack on the Pentagon."

"Great," I said, "that sounds wonderful. But for a moment there I thought you said it will be the season opener, September 11, national TV, with a special tribute to families of victims of the Pentagon attack."

"Exactly."

"Oh."

The man added that Nick Lachey and Jessica Simpson would he singing with me, and that eased my anxiety a bit, knowing I could kind of blend into the background behind the superstars. I didn't learn until game day that Nick and Jessica would sing 20 minutes earlier, from the grandstands, and the National Anthem would be performed at midfield by old Roy, all by his lonesome.

I flew to D.C. with my then 15-year-old son Andy. He had his own football game Friday night, so we caught a redeye, got to D.C. early Saturday and went sightseeing. It was Andy's first trip to Washington and I was the proud-dad tour-guide. Late in the day it occurred to me that maybe I should he giving some thought to the Anthem.

I'm on stage just about every week, singing and performing, but this was different. Really, though, how tough could it be? It's the National Anthem, I've been singing it since I was four.

Kickoff was 1 p.m. Sunday and we got to the stadium about 9:30 a.m. The field was already a hubbub of activity and Andy was busy looking around and getting autographs from players who came out early to loosen up.

I did a run-through of the song and told the sound guy I was having trouble hearing myself because the sound was bouncing all over the stadium. "Don't worry," he said, "when the fans fill the seats, the acoustics change and the sound won't bounce."

I knew that wasn't completely true. Even in a full stadium, the sound of your voice comes out of the loudspeakers and back to you about a week later, You're on "by the dawn's early" and suddenly all you can hear is your voice singing "Oh – o say can you see!" it's like singing in the round with yourself, row-row-row-your-boat, only you forget which of the three voices is the live you. Fortunately, you have a sound monitor in front of you that helps you focus on your live voice.

"By the way, Roy" the sound guy told me, "we're not gonna be able to have a sound monitor on the field."

Oh.

Nick and Jessica did their thing, they were great, and then it was my turn. As I took my place at midfield I looked up and gulped. There is nothing, not even singing for 35,000 at a baseball game, that prepares you for 80,000 people, stacked seemingly into the distant clouds, standing and waiting for you to sing a song written for a goose.

I don't read a lot of psychology textbooks, but I'm sure there is a clinical condition called something like National Anthem Anxiety.

"I know there's no chance I could forget the lyrics," I told myself. "But I wonder if there's a place I can write 'em down, just in case, where nobody would notice. I could put a little cue card by my shoes, but how would I see it if I needed it? You don't want someone saying, "Mr. Patriot, on the anniversary of September 11, used cue cards for the National Anthem." Maybe I could drop to one knee, like Al Jolson, and sneak, a peek? No, probably not."

Because your brain loves to play games, create a thousand tragic scenarios. The brain loves to casually muse, "Is it gleaming, or is it streaming? Is streaming first, then gleaming, or is there no streaming at all? Do trout gleam in a steam?"

Then the brain calls up a catalogue of past. National Anthem disasters and debacles, Carl Lewis waaay off-key. Glen Campbell, Robert Goulet and so many others forgetting the words. That little girl going blank at midcourt, bailed out by then Trail Blazers coach Maurice Cheeks. Frank Sinatra missing notes by six feet. Sinatra is the greatest singer of the 20th century, yet many sports fans remember him best for his croaking Anthem before a Dodger game, re-played a million times on L.A., radio stations.

Maybe a mental check-list would calm me down:

- Easy song, I've sung it a thousand times in front of audiences.
- Got the lyrics down cold, and just in case I've got this discreet
  gleaming-streaming cheat-sheet of key words.
- The fans are friendly and are barely paying attention to me, they're ready for the game.
- Potential to offend families of the September 11 tragedy, make a fool of myself before national TV audience, and humiliate my teenage son.

I picture 80,000 fans who have been breakfasting on Budweiser and Johnny Walker, booing and mocking Andy's father. That was the scary part. I wanted to show Andy that in some small way his father is capable of doing something that doesn't involve re-takes, edits and second chances. This is live theater. Can dad handle the pressure?

"And now," the PA man said, "to sing our National Anthem... Roy Firestone."

Strange crowd reaction. It was kind of a gasp, like, "Huhhh?" As in, "Roy Firestone, the TV sports guy? Why him?"

I'm thinking, "You better hit that first note, pal, or you're in big trouble."

I hit it, but got to "say" and here comes the giant echo of the beginning of the song. I told myself, "Screw it, just sing straight ahead, don't listen to anything."

There was a lot going on. The names of the victims of the Pentagon attack were scrolling on the message board. The giant 500-foot-flag was waving. The players, eager to get started, were shifting and twitching. The sea of faces. Andy was standing eight feet away and I decided I'd just look into his eyes and sing.

At "Oh, say does," the jets roared over, and I mean roared. The stadium shook, the ground shook, and I could hear nothing. I just kept singing.

Then it was over. I had survived.

As I walked off the field, LaVar Arrington said, "Hey, man, I didn't know you could sing."

When I got to Andy he stuck up his hand and gave me the first high-five he's ever given me and said, in his newly-deep teenage voice, "Good job, Dad. You didn't blow it."

Best review I ever got.

Christopher Reeve

Man of Steel.

SUPER
MAN

*This is a letter I wrote to my kids the
night Christopher Reeve died.*

Dear Andy and Nicky:

It's late at night and I'm sitting here remembering one of my heroes, a man I'd like you to know about.

He played Superman in the movies, and then when real life dealt him a cruel blow, he became a very real Superman, not just an actor. His name, as you might know, was Christopher Reeve, but what you might not know about him is that in addition to being a great actor and famous movie star, he was an athlete. At Cornell University he was an outstanding hockey goalie, and he was an active sailor and a horseman, until he was thrown from a horse and suffered a near-fatal spinal injury that left him paralyzed from the neck down.

This Superman who flew, like a speeding bullet and bent steel in his bare hands in the movies, spent the last nine years of his life unable to use his body, unable to so much as bend a finger. But he became even more of a Superman than the character he played on screen.

I want to share with you something I heard him say, and someday it might mean more to you than it will now. He said, "I have a bigger problem with able-bodied people in life who are paralyzed... The people who stay in the shallow part of the pool, who can't move ahead in life because they are afraid or angry or feel incapable of trying something that they never tried before. They are the real tragic figures."

As you go through life, remember that because things are hard and scary and seem impossible doesn't mean they should prevent you from moving forward. What they should do is help you achieve more than you ever dreamed you could.

Don't allow yourselves to become paralyzed. Don't let hate or fear or sadness or lack of confidence ruin your life. Not every man is as courageous as Christopher Reeve, who fought intense pain and battled the limits of his will and his mind and became a true hero. But every man can overcome "impossible" hurdles.

Live every day of your life with a sense of purpose, even if the purpose is to enjoy simple pleasures. A laugh. A song. A breath of fresh air.

And never, ever, no matter how hard or challenging life becomes, allow you goodness to be broken! Do good every day, in word and in deed! When your money runs out or your business fails or your friends seem far away, when your hopes and dreams seem impossible, you will always have your spirit. You will not be invincible, because there is no real Superman, but your spirit can always help you rise up and overcome. Your spirit is stronger than you know.

And every day you will move forward with something more important than wealth or fame or possessions – a sense of yourselves. You will have pride and a self-satisfaction that you tried to be the best person you could be, the person God wants you to be.

That is my hope. That is my sincerest wish.

Love,
Dad

With John Wooden

With Jim Brown

With Mike Tyson

Three walking definitions of true athletic greatness.

chapter 10

MY ALL-TALK
ALL-STAR TEAM

I propose a toast to all the folks who have taken the time through the years to sit down with me and share their lives with you. Without them, my career would have been very lonely.

I can't honor them all, and it would be impossible to crown a Best Interview, but I'll gladly hand out some awards here to my own personal all-star team:

Most Introspective: *Arthur Ashe*

The man could, and always did, go deep, really give you every ounce of his heart. Smartest person I've ever talked to. I'd also give Ashe my award for Most Respected.

Most Sage: *John Wooden*

Truly a wizard. Being with the Coach is like hanging with the Dalai Lama, and Wooden is a very nice man.

Most Honest: *Charles Barkley*

Incapable of hiding his true feelings. Or maybe it's just that Charles has too much fun telling the flat-out truth as he feels it.

Wittiest: *Jim Valvano and Fred Dryer*

This one's a tie.

Most Street-Smart: *Allen Iverson*

I hate to say it, but I was expecting to dislike Allen before our first interview. He fooled me. He always manages to charm, to be interesting, compelling and fascinating.

Now That I Think About It, As Street Smart as Iverson: *Howie Long*

Incredibly quick wit, and a great storyteller. Despite his glossy TV resume, Howie is still the kid from Boston's inner city and from the NFL's grittiest trenches.

Best Personal Turnaround: *Mickey Mantle*

I'm told Mickey was a jerk during his playing days. But he grew and he changed. When Mantle owned up to, and attacked, his alcoholism, he became one of the best, warmest guys I've ever known. More importantly, he became an activist, using his power and celebrity to help other people, working hard to promote organ-transplant and organ-donor programs. Heroism is the ability to do one's very best in a crisis, and I believe Mickey became a true hero late in his life, much more so than when he was hitting 500-foot home runs.

Best Dressed: *Dennis Rodman*

Hey, this is show biz, and nobody understands that better than Rodman and his wardrobe team.

Most Himself: *Tom Brady*

He's exactly what he seems to be, a very nice and very consistent man. Tom is always seems happy to be here, always having a very good day and glad to be sharing it with you. Brady loved telling me the story about how his dad took him to see the 49ers-Cowboys in the playoffs, the game of The Catch, the famous Joe Montana-to-Dwight Clark play. Tom and his dad missed The Catch because Tom was crying because his father wouldn't buy him a foam "No. 1" finger.

Most Relevant: *Jim Brown*

Most kids today know nothing of Jim Brown the football hero, but thousands of young people's lives are being impacted in a positive way by Brown's on-going work with inner-city gangs. He's much tougher and more dangerous now than when he was busting up linebackers. Incredibly intense.

Most Charming: *Chris Webber*

He's made a lot of mistakes and yet Webber is one of the smartest guys I've interviewed. A great converser, always honest (except about the Michigan stuff) and thoughtful.

Most Combative: *Frank Robinson*

I've known Frank since I was 15 and he hasn't changed a bit. Always looking for a fight, but a good one, and I really admire him. At 70, when Robinson could be on the golf course, he was where he loved to be – in the trenches, managing a ballclub. Never backs down.

Least Likely to Whine: *Grant Hill*

Not that he's had a horrible life, but Grant's career has been one long injury, and he has faced every painful step with quiet courage, dignity, resolve, never a whimper.

Most At Home in the Spotlight: *Tommy Lasorda*

He needs the attention, loves it, responds to it, creates it. And say what you will about Tommy, the man can tell a story.

Most Elegant: *David Robinson*

Enormous dignity, great compassion.

Mr. Bring-it-on: *Phil Mickelson*

Rain or shine, a good guy to talk to. I never feel he is protected by anybody, never has his guard up. Lefty has his demons, he's had his failures, and he always discusses them with candor.

Closest to Royalty, Without the Pomp: *Arnold Palmer*

When Arnold walks into a room, people snap to attention, although he always manages to put everyone at ease.

Favorite Guy's Guy: *Steve Young*

A great mixture of good humor and high intensity. Steve has an innate ability to look unimportant, just another schlub in the room. Some interview subjects answer your questions, but it's as if they were in some sort of isolation bubble. Steve engages in conversation, he connects. It's never just about him.

Deepest Well of Opinions and Thoughts: *Wilt Chamberlain*

He was on the show dozens of times and was never boring. Wilt had a unique style, and for such a big and intimidating man, he was very much a teddy bear. He always felt comfortable on the show, and he always brought a great presence, and I truly miss the guy.

Flat-Out Goofiest: *Randall "Tex" Cobb*

Funny, outrageous, and I'm sure he would admit now that there were times he came on the show coked to the gills. A hillbilly philosopher, party animal and good-time brawler.

Least Likely to Phone It In: *Terry Bradshaw*

Incapable of giving you a bad interview. Loves the format, loves talking, loves people, and his well-publicized demons make him all the more interesting.

Most Likely to Make You Shake Your Head: *Mike Tyson*

Never the same guy twice, but always a compelling interview. Can be crass and boorish, or erudite and philosophical. Can discuss Legs Diamond, Aristotle, pigeons or politics. Utterly fascinating.

Best Antidote for a Slow Day: *Reggie Jackson*

Nobody flips the switch on like Reggie. He can, and will, talk about everything, is never cheated out of his verbal swings. Even when he's hostile, Reggie is great live theater.

Still My Idol: *Brooks Robinson*

As a kid in Miami I was a spring-training batboy for the Orioles and Brooks would always play pepper with me. A champion then and a champion always.

Most Politically Correct: *Cal Ripken Jr.*

I believe Cal prides himself in editing his thoughts to carefully avoid even the slightest whiff of controversy. Doesn't always make for the liveliest of interviews, but there's something so straightforward and ethical about Cal that I can't help but admire him and enjoy his company.

Most Like Your Old Loosey Goosey High School Buddy: *Brett Favre*

Incredibly comfortable with himself and with just about everyone else – teammates, media, you name it. I'm talking to him in a hotel lobby one day and a man comes up and says, "You look like Brett Favre." Brett says, "Yeah, I get that all the time. I'm actually his twin brother, Darrell." The guy asks for an autograph anyway and Brett signs it, "Best wishes, Darrell Favre."

Most Radiant Smile: *Magic Johnson*

Now and forever.

Most Genuinely Off-Center: *Fred Dryer*

A certified five-star interview, never fails to knock me off my chair. Once you get Fred going, just move aside and let the freight train through. Hilarious, amusing, unconventional, thoughtful.

Most Like Himself: *Jack Nicholson*

Jack's not really an actor, he's just a guy who shows up on the set and plugs in one of his crazy actual personalities. We sat together on a plane flight home from a fight, we talked about betting on the fight, I asked him how much he bet. "Let me put it to you this way," he said. "Whatever it was to me, it was like a dime to you." A very unusual mind. A woman approached Jack in a nightclub once and asked, "Wanna dance?" Nicholson shot back, "Wrong verb."

Most Sincere: *Larry Brown*

Not capable of lying, wears his heart on his sleeve, is like a walking soap opera. Very likeable and fascinating guy.

Most Strangely Compelling: *Pete Rose*

He may be a liar, but Pete is so convincing that I think he convinces himself. A genuine two-fisted guy who has a strong opinion about everything and is always fired up for a conversation. Incidentally, doesn't Pete seem like less of a serial killer now that so many other baseball players have been exposed as steroid cheats?

Most At Home in the Guest Chair: *Barry Bonds*

That's the old Barry, not the current recluse. Barry will probably never do the show again, because times have changed and he has retreated into a cave, but he used to be a wonderful guest – humorous, thoughtful, sensitive. He just sat down and poured out his heart, opened up his soul.

Most Dramatic: *Hubie Brown*

When Hubie talked about his father (see Chapter 3), he went into a virtual trance, it was the most intensely emotional interview I've been part of.

Mr. Not-Mr.-Hollywood: *Samuel L. Jackson*

He's a former college revolutionary, former crack addict. He's one of Hollywood's top-grossing actors, but Jackson told me he approaches every acting job as if he's still looking for his first paycheck, as hungry as when he was driving a cab. Very likeable man.

Most Aware of the Medium: *Jimmy Johnson*

Very outspoken, loves controversy, loves to explain how he can out-coach and out-think you. Jimmy enjoys every moment in the sun.

Most Coachable: *Alex Rodriguez*

I interviewed A-Rod very early in his career, his first big national interview, and he was nervous. He called me Mr. Firestone. I asked him to comment on a controversy involving Robby Alomar, and Alex gave me a deer-in-headlights look. He didn't want to defend Robby, but he didn't want to publicly attack his friend, either. He said to me on-camera, "Can we have a time-out?" I just looked at him, and he said, "Can we turn the camera off and talk, please?" Then he asked me, "How would you answer this question? Frankly, I'm a little intimidated here. Can you give me an idea?" I gave him some suggestions, we re-started the taping and Alex said, "While I can't condone..." He said word-for-word what I had just said to him. After the session he whispered to me, "I won't tell anybody if you don't."

Most Surreal: *Richard Nixon*

Throughout our interview I couldn't shake the thought, "I'm talking serious baseball with Richard Milhous Nixon."

Favorite Interview:

Okay, I can pick one favorite. My dad.

With Donald Trump

What a charming guy... except for the interview.

BORES AND BAD BOYS

Father Flanagan once said, "There's no such thing as a bad boy."

Well there is such thing as a bad interview subject. They are fairly rare, because if you enjoy interviewing as much as I do, you embrace the good, the bad and the ugly, variety being the spice of entertainment.

But there are a few people who, if I never sit down with 'em again, it will be too soon. Here are my Exercise In Futility All-Stars:

Most Dangerous: *Albert Belle*

I didn't even trick-or-treat at his house, and Albert still scared me (see Chapter 7).

Biggest Jerk: *Deion Sanders*

Even after his evolution, becoming a devout Christian, Neon Deion is still the same old jerk. Really strange dude. Blew me off several times, which doesn't make him a bad guy, but the last time he said he'd do the show, my crew waited several hours and he stiffed us again. Is it selling out to keep your word?

Least Comfortable On Camera: *Mark McGwire*

This is no surprise to anyone who saw the Congressional hearings, but even on a little interview show, Mark is ill-a-tease. Never trustful of, or comfortable with, the media.

Rudest: *Howard Cosell*

Red Smith once wrote, "I have tried to like Howard Cosell and I have failed." Many of us were in that boat. Howard was a journalistic icon, a brilliant and principled man, but what a pompous pain in the tush.

Most Disappointing: *Bill Russell*

Boy, I wanted to like this guy, for all he's accomplished and endured, and for all he claims to stand for. But I failed. This is a man who, on principle, wouldn't sign autographs for his own teammates, and now charges $700 per signature at autograph shows. I don't want to throw too many honors Russell's way, but I'd also rate him Most Condescending.

Biggest Boor: *Donald Trump*

You'd think with all that money the Donald could buy some charm and warmth. I didn't like the way Trump treated my crew, I didn't like his attitude during the interview. Arrogant, abrasive, condescending, vain – and he'll probably consider this a compliment.

Most Elusive: *Tiger Woods*

He's made a career out of avoiding interviews, and not just with me. Several times we'd set up an interview, only to have it cancelled. Sorry, Tiger has to fly to Scotland. Sorry, something came up. He's the greatest athlete of his generation, but even when he does an interview, he doesn't give much. Maybe the most reclusive and carefully-self-edited star in sports.

Most Not Worth the Effort: *Michael Jordan*

Again, not a bad person. And somewhere in there is a very interesting guy. But Michael has always been aware that he doesn't need the media exposure. He never tried to really engage, because he didn't need to. At one end of the interview spectrum you have people pouring out their hearts and souls. At the other end you have people like Woods and Jordan.

Don't Bother: *Ken Griffey, Jr.*

He never met a reporter, interviewer or photographer he liked. Wary, insecure, hostile, disrespectful. Very ill-at-ease in front of a TV camera.

Not Mr. Warmth: *Randy Johnson*

I don't think the Big Unit likes anything about being a celebrity, except maybe the money. One of the most exciting pitchers in history, but put him in front of a camera and the excitement drains away.

Least Reliable: *Darryl Strawberry*

Maybe it was the drugs talking, but you could always count on not being able to count on Darryl.

Arm's Length Award: *Dan Marino*

I know, on TV he's charming, talkative and fun. But during his career, when he was asked to do interviews with me or any media, he ran the gamut from barely-accessible to kiss-my-pigskin.

Oral Hygiene Award: *Eddie Murray*

I once spoke to him briefly in front of his locker. He was brushing his teeth and he didn't even bother to remove the brush to talk to me. I think Eddie used the glowering, menacing front to keep the world at a distance. It worked.

With Barry Bonds

Before the strangeness.

chapter 12

THE MYSTERIOUS MR. BONDS

The best opening act I've ever had for my stand-up show is a comedian named Barry Lamar Bonds. I'll tell you about the night he opened for me, but first let's talk about the mystery of Barry Bonds.

The mystery is how a phenomenal athlete with good looks, a 1,000-watt smile, a (sometimes) charming and gregarious personality, a sense of humor, and more athletic talent than anyone else in his game, has made himself into the nation's most disliked athlete.

I realize there's room for debate on that title. Dennis Rodman and John Rocker are two villains who spring to mind. They were disliked but they were like cartoons. Rodman didn't become truly goofy and a detriment to his teams until his career was winding down, and Rocker was never really important enough to rate a national bad guy title.

Some are misunderstood or feared. Jim Brown still intimidates people. Bobby Knight scares people, too, but others see him as a John Wayne-type tough guy.

Barry Bonds isn't intimidating, scary, goofy or irrelevant. He is disliked. I run into very few people outside the Bay Area who like Barry even a little.

Granted, most of these people don't know Barry except through the media, but Bonds has some control over the media. He's got his own web site and he had his own TV reality show, essentially showcasing his best side, but it didn't really work.

And it's not just the faceless public failing to warm to Bonds. A lot of fans didn't like Deion Sanders, but most of his teammates, in football and baseball, adored the guy. You watch Bonds at the ballpark and he's an island, isolated, his personal section of the clubhouse seemingly off-limits to everyone but his crew of personal trainers.

The steroid scandal hurt Bonds, no question, but that kind of taint doesn't have to be fatal, Jason Giambi was publicly outed as a steroid abuser, he apologized, however vaguely, and was returned to the good graces of the fans, even those outside New York.

Some say racism is a factor in Barry's unpopularity, but a lot of the same people who love Tiger Woods and Dwyane Wade and Clinton Portis hate Barry. Racism can never be discounted, but it's not a major reason Barry is disliked.

I believe Barry achieved the title of America's Most Hated Jock the hard way: He earned it.

Here's a true story: A man who worked closely with Bonds on one of his media projects told Bonds, "Listen, Barry, a lot of people don't like you, there's even a perception that Hank (Aaron) doesn't like you. How about if I donate $50,000 from my production company and you match it? We'll announce that Barry Bonds is donating $100,000 to Hank Aaron's Chasing a Dream Foundation. We'll fly Hank to San Francisco and you present him a giant check at home plate before a game. It will be a great thing to show what kind of person you are, Hank will be happy and the press will have a feel-good story."

Barry's response: "Why the f#*% do I gotta give $50,000?"

Buddy Hackett once said of Howard Cosell, "There's a split opinion on Howard. Some people hate him like poison, and some people just hate him regular."

That's Barry Bonds, but it hasn't always been this way. He's always been quirky and had a prima donna side, but I remember back when Bonds wasn't the villain he is today.

Like the night he opened for me.

It was 1997, I was in Atlanta to perform my stand up act for an illustrious sports audience at a show put on by Franklin Sports. Franklin was celebrating its 50th year in business and they had all their big endorsement athletes in the audience, people like Dan Marino, Sugar Ray Leonard and Tony Gwynn.

I was ready to go on and the audience was restless and distracted. It had been a long program already, and now there was a technical problem with the video screen. I was waiting near the stage and Bonds sidled up.

"You want me to get them quiet, Roy?" he asked.

"What do you have in mind, Barry?"

He said, "Watch this."

As God is my witness, Barry Bonds, the man many now see as a social misfit and humorless recluse, grabbed my microphone and did 20 minutes of improv stand-up comedy. He killed. Barry had 'em rolling.

He was doing Arsenio Hall-type stuff, just riffing. Herschel Walker was there and Barry said, "Ever notice how Herschel runs? He never looks like he's moving because he's got this big ass," and Barry did an impression of Walker running.

The crowd loved it.

He did impressions of baseball players' stances. Hilarious. He walked around goofing on everyone, working that huge VIP room for 20 minutes! It occurred to me that maybe Barry is truly in his element only when he has a stick in his hand and he's the center of attention. Give him a bat or a microphone, and a full house and the spotlight, and he's home.

Barry is one of my favorite athletes to deal with, and one of my least favorites. He can be open and engaging, but when he's in a foul mood, which seems to be most of the time these days, he is not fun. I was in his inner circle for a while, we did several long TV interviews together and talked often, and I once told him, "Barry, if you look at it from a purely cynical viewpoint, it would be profitable for you to be a good guy. Just be a good guy!"

But he equated being a good guy to being phony, selling out. The irony is that when he's the badass, people see him as a phony.

They want to believe that the gruff and bitter Barry isn't the real Barry. I'm not sure Barry knows who the real Barry is.

His public image is a train wreck and was even before the steroid stuff. This is a guy with an uncanny knack for offending people and not giving a damn.

"I can be an ass," Barry once told me in an interview, "I'm not ever gonna say I couldn't be an ass. I can be the best."

He reminds me of Reggie Jackson and Howard Cosell, two guys who were immensely talented and charming, who loved the spotlight, but alienated the public. Reggie and Howard always knew exactly what they were doing, everything was premeditated, however offensive. With Barry, it comes naturally.

Barry and I got pretty close in the late '90s and I think he trusted me, as much as he trusts anybody. He was very open in our interviews. We talked about his father, Bobby, with whom he didn't have a great relationship as a kid. It was the first time he addressed that issue publicly and that was a little tense, but I think Barry was glad we did it. He broke down and cried on camera when he was telling me the story of his grandfather's death, how he gave Barry the cross that he now wears as an earring.

Bonds has a rep for not being much of a teammate, for barely knowing the guys on his team, but he seems to have made connection with at least a few over the years. He once told me about his friendship with a Giants' relief pitcher.

"You know," Barry said in one of our interviews, "the person that I love more than anyone on my team is Robb Nen. Robb Nen unconditionally is my friend, because he will allow me to be an ass, he'll allow me to be nice, and he has the same respect for me. He's like, 'Hi, Barry,' and I don't wanna talk to him that day 'cause I'm trying to focus on the game, and he's like, 'Hi, Barry,' he'll tease me. 'Hi, Barry. Hi, Barry.' He knows it's irritating me and he doesn't care…And he brings out the soft side of me that is very rare to come out…Robb Nen, I love that man, I love him to death, I think he's one of the best guys in baseball."

That's a glimpse of the human side, but there's also the chemical side, and we'll probably never know the whole story there. I don't know if Barry did 'roids, but he gave my viewers a plausible explanation for his improving so dramatically as a hitter at a late stage of his career. This is from a 2002 interview and Barry is talking about something he learned, an almost Zen-like breakthrough he had recently experienced.

"I can miss a pitch, and it's like something in my head, or this visual impact of how I swung the time I did hit a home run a previous time, all of a sudden that comes back into my visual. And so I can get on-deck (before the next at-bat), and I can re-position myself back into that position. That's something I couldn't do before, and I can't understand why I'm able to do that now when I couldn't before."

Bonds hit 73 homers in 2001, and I flew to Houston when he was at 69. The Astros' manager, Larry Dierker, basically ordered his pitchers not to throw a ball anywhere near the strike zone to Bonds. So there was controversy and tension in the air.

There were at least 200 reporters and 200 photographers on the field during batting practice, all of them with one target – Barry Bonds. As I walked onto the field I heard Bonds call out, "Roy, come over here!" Bonds is white-hot but he is granting interviews to nobody, he is keeping the media at a long arm's length.

"Roy, come over here for a sec!"

He put an arm around my shoulders and started talking to me, and I felt pretty special. The man of the hour had singled me out. Then he whispered in my ear, "You know why I have my arm around you?"

"No, why?"

"Because none of these photographers want a picture of you and me together. They just want me. If you're here they can't get a picture."

So he kept his arm around my shoulders for several minutes, using me as a human shield. It's the closest I ever came to feeling like a cheap floozy.

When Bonds' body changed, when he got huge in 2000, gained about 35 pounds that winter, I saw him in spring training in Yuma and I said, "Geez, you got fat!" And he said, "This isn't fat, Roy, this is all muscle." He didn't even look like the Barry Bonds. He couldn't even pass for Barry's big brother. He was a cartoon, he looked like one of those monster trucks on ESPN.

Barry said to me, "You know what I'm going to do, Roy? I'm going to break some records that are never going to be broken again, and the first one I'm going to break is my godfather's (Willie Mays) home-run record."

Until then, Barry's biggest homer season was '93 when he hit 46. In 2000 the New Barry hit 49, and the next season, at age 37(!), he hit 73.

Now he says that the homer records don't matter to him, but I remember vividly the determination in Barry's voice that spring when he told me he was going to rewrite the homerun records. I believe, as the authors speculated in *Game of Shadows*, that Bonds was resentful of the attention going to lesser ballplayers who were jacked up on juice.

Bonds decided to play catch-up, and whatever he did seems to have obliterated what humanity he had. It's sad, because some day he will wake up and realize that life is about friendship and affection and appreciating who you are and giving back. Remember the echo? Life is an echo, you get back what you send out.

If Barry ever gets that wake-up call, it will have to come from within, because I don't think anybody gets to Barry, nobody has his ear. Friends call friends on their b.s., that's one of the most important duties of friendship, and I don't believe Barry has that kind of friend. There are many people flitting around him, but he's alone.

He reminds me of Mickey Mantle, whose personal shortcomings were largely hidden from the public, but Mickey was a hero with serious personal flaws. As he neared death, Mantle finally let the world in, admitted he needed people and decided he wanted to be a better human being.

Bonds might someday realize he hasn't been nice to people, and that he has hurt the game that gave him so much. Pete Rose said to me, "I broke the cardinal rule of baseball by gambling, but I never tried to cheat the records, never tried to do anything on the field except play hard." And Pedro Martinez told me, "You know, the thing I'm proudest of is that I faced the best the game ever had and I know that I pitched clean, never used steroids or enhancements, never took greenies. That's a satisfaction I have when I look in the mirror."

I wonder if Barry wonders what part of his career is real, and what part of Barry Bonds is real.

With Lance Armstrong

Cancer's worst enemy.

chapter
13

LANCE, DANCING

There are many electrifying calls in sports, like the stretch run of the Kentucky Derby, the knockout punch of a championship fight, and almost any great moment called by Vin Scully.

But for poetry and goosebumps, I'll never forget the TV announcer's call in 2006 when I was watching Lance Armstrong go for his seventh straight Tour de France victory. The race had entered the Alps, a brutal stretch where the riders seemed to be laboring straight up an asphalt cliff. The BBC announcer cried out, as only a BBC announcer can cry out, "And here's Lance Armstrong, dancing on the pedals!"

How could you more beautifully describe a man's career, his monumental achievement, his dominance?

We often talk about athletes overcoming obstacles. I have a small quibble with that phrase. Often, I believe, athletes don't so much overcome obstacles, but, as Lance Armstrong did in surviving cancer, they use the obstacles to forge a stronger character, allowing them to exceed their previous limitations.

It sounds crazy, but Lance will tell you he needed cancer, he used cancer. This is a man who can, without a trace of irony, use the phrase "the beauty of my illness." His illness: at age 29, he had 14 tumors in his body, in a testicle, brain and lungs. The treatment included brain surgery.

"The illness really taught me to thrive, in sports and in life," Armstrong told me after his seventh and final Tour win. "I never would have won the Tour de France without the disease, without the illness, without the struggle, without those lessons that I learned in three or four short months.

"What people forget is, I was a racer before my illness, and I wasn't bad. In the year I was diagnosed, I was the No. 1 rider in the world for a good part of the year. I won the world championship in 1993, which made me, I think, the youngest world champion. So I had a career in the works.

"But through the illness I said, 'Okay, this is my life. I've been given my chance and I'm going to do everything I can to capitalize on it.'"

Cancer made Lance one bad dude, even gave him the fortitude to shut out the bizarre rumors and allegations about his alleged drug use. One book claimed that Armstrong never had cancer, that his cancer story was a phony cover for his alleged use of performance-enhancing drugs. The author of that book obviously wasn't there in Houston the day a doctor pulled Lance's mother aside and told her, "We don't think your son's going to make it."

Cancer made Lance what he is today – a seven-time Tour de France champ and, more importantly, one of the world's most powerful fighters in the war on cancer. His Lance Armstrong Foundation raises money and awareness. This is how Lance cashes in on his fame: He took a bike ride with President Bush and told him, "We need a billion dollars for cancer."

Bono of the rock group U2 said in *Sports Illustrated*, "Lance is different. He understands that hills can be climbed, and he isn't even depressed when, upon reaching the summit of one, he sees a larger one. He's used to that."

Lance is still attacking the mountains, still dancing on the pedals.

I had a chance to sit down twice with Lance soon after his final Tour win and subsequent retirement, if you can call his current 24/7 anti-cancer campaign retirement. Here are some highlights from our chats:

In your book you write that if you could go back and have a choice between winning the Tour de France and having cancer, you'd take the cancer. What do you mean by that?

It's true. Winning the Tour, winning any event, changes life temporarily, but won't change life forever, and the illness did that for me, it changed my life, my perspective on life, forever. Winning the Tour, you get a nice jersey, a nice trophy, endorsements.

But without the illness, the Tour wouldn't have happened. Well, I suppose I would have ridden the Tour again, but the victories wouldn't have happened.

You're saying that without the cancer, you don't win the Tour de France?

Exactly. Without the illness, the shock, the process of going through treatments, the process of finding a cure, what I learned about myself, what I learned about my potential as a person, as a man, as an athlete.

Without the illness, I wouldn't have learned to focus on my life. I learned to focus on the specifics of cycling, the diet, the training, the preparation, the technology, the innovation, the building of a team. The illness really taught me how to build the best team possible, because I was forced to find the best doctors, the best nurses, the best hospitals, the best procedures.

You very much took charge of the process.

It was a crash course – one week (to study and make a decision on a location and course of treatment). *This was back in '96. Now you can get on the Web and learn a lot about your illness immediately. Back then it wasn't that easy, it took a long time.*

Do you feel that you whipped cancer, or that it was just dumb luck?

I think I had amazing doctors, I know that. I like to think I have an amazing attitude, I wanted badly to live, I wasn't ready to die. But I truly believe that I had the best doctors in the word and I looked long and hard for them. I was diagnosed in Austin (his home town) *and started treatment in Austin. I felt that I was getting a lot of pressure to go to the hospital in Austin, which is one of the best cancer hospitals in the world.*

I spent an afternoon there and just said, 'You know, it doesn't feel right.' I went to the airport and bought a one-way ticket to Indianapolis, met with doctors there (Indiana University) *and thought, 'This is the right place.' Just like you'd take your kid around to find a college – here's the campus, here's the dorms – it was just like that. I went with my mom and a friend, and it was literally like trying to choose an education and make a major decision.*

Within a week. And when I go there I said, 'This is it, this is my place, I believe in these guys. I believe that if I have any chance at all, it's here.' And that's the best you can hope for, that you've done everything you can. If it doesn't work out you can die knowing that you did everything you could.

I started treatment in Austin with standard therapy, which included a drug called bleomycin, which is a very tough drug (one side effect is severe and permanent lung damage). *I did one cycle of the drug there, and when I went to Indiana they switched me to a regimen that didn't have this drug. They said, 'We think you might want to race again, and if you take four cycles of bleomycin, you'll never be on a bike again ever, guaranteed.'*

The question was, do I mind being an in-patient for three or four months? Because with the new regime, you're hooked up to the IV all the time, you're treated four to six hours a day and the rest of the time you're on hydration.

So they said, 'Do you want to be an out-patient with the other regime, or do you want to be an in-patient with this new regime that we think can preserve your career?' I said, 'Look, guys, I just want to live.' They said, 'We think you can live, so let's do that.' Without that decision in Indiana, I never would have ridden again. They believed in it, these guys. But I was told in certain places, 'We just don't think you're going to make it' I mean, it was about 50-50.

People depict you as a courageous man. Are you, or were you at times a frightened man, a man who didn't want to battle?

The word courage is a serious word. I would like to think that at those times I was very courageous and that I wanted to win and wanted to live, but there are millions of people like that. There are 75 million adult women battling breast cancer, and they're incredibly courageous.

But they have their moments, just like I did, when you get a little bit of bad news, especially in the beginning of my illness, and every week there was something new that came along, those moments when you think, 'Jesus, when is this going to end, and is it going to end in victory or defeat?' The key is to stay predominantly positive, I mean in the high 90s.

At one point with Dr. Larry Einhorn in Indiana, you were reading your charts, you saw your HEG count, right? And a dangerously high HEG count is between 60 and 70, and you said, 'I think it says my count is 180.' And he said, 'Well, that's a little high.' And you said, 'What is the K for?' and he said, 'Your count is 180 thousand.'

I was either very sick or very pregnant. I would have rather been pregnant.

Francis Ford Coppola once said that if you have a great idea, and you're trying to do something with it, and nobody ever tries to tell you that what you're trying to do is stupid, it's not a great idea. At any point, did anyone tell you that what you were trying to do, beat cancer and get back to racing, was not a smart thing to do?

Well, the beauty of the illness is that it allowed me to live my life with no expectations. I was truly the underdog. I was the guy that wasn't given an opportunity to come back. I remember it now as a great challenge.

When I joined the U.S. Postal Service in 1998, they had the worst team in the division, it was crazy to think we could become the best team in the world. In the beginning it was a joke.

And that was an interesting time, starting from nothing, and it was a very useful and very safe place for me to be. When I was in the hospital, just after brain surgery (two cancer lesions were removed from his brain), *Chris, my coach, came in and said, 'How are you doing?' And I said, 'I'm doing great!' And he kind of laughed because he was thinking I must really be drugged up. He had no idea what was going on.*

And I said, 'No, Chris, I'm doing great.' And we back and forth, like, 'Are you really *doing great?' 'Yeah, Chris, you don't understand, I'm at the lowest point in my life, it can only get better.' And that is an incredibly powerful position to be in.*

There were heroes everywhere you looked. You were essentially uninsured, and your sponsors stepped in?

I had been sponsored by Oakley (sunglasses) *for a long time, still am, and they told their insurance company, 'He's our employee, and you either insure him or lose the company* (Oakley account). *You can choose.'*

Think of all the people that don't have that kind of clout.

It happens all the time. The fight is incredibly complicated, incredibly expensive, incredibly hard to navigate for somebody who is not prepared for that, which nobody really is, and we know people miss getting treatment because they can't afford it.

And a lot of times, it's the people who never had a chance in the first place, they're from the poorest neighborhoods, with the worst crime and drug problems, and when they're down (with cancer), *they don't have the opportunity to live. That has to change.*

The yellow wrist bands, you've sold how many?

About 60 million.

Was the band your idea?

All my idea (laugh). *Nike actually made these bands before, they called 'em 'ballers,' Some Nike guys were sitting around a table with me and said, 'Let's take a baller and make it yellow and put "Live Strong" on it. And well make five million of 'em* (for 10 cents each) *and we'll give 'em to you, and if they're not all sold, we'll just give you $5 million* (for Armstrong's charity).'

I said, 'You guys are nuts, you'll never get rid of five million of these things.' And sure enough, we went through the five quick, the

Tour happened, and the Olympics, where so many athletes were nice
enough to wear 'em while competing, athletes from all over the world,
and things just went crazy. A year and a half later, 60 million.

What's a stronger power in the universe – fear or love?

In my universe, as an athlete, I was always fear-based. I was
always worried that I was gonna lose, worried I was gonna let the
fans down, and sponsors and supporters.

Worried that you would die?

Worried that I would die, certainly.

Still worried?

Uh, I didn't worry about it today, but I sure respect it. If I started
to feel funny, I would be back at the doctor so fast. I respect this
illness like nothing else, it is a total and complete bastard, so I'm
not turning my back on it, ever.

I would be remiss not to acknowledge the most important
influence in your life, your mother, Linda. She wrote a book, too,
and it happens to be a best-seller. What did you learn from this
woman?

Well, I learned a simple lesson: Don't ever give up. I don't know
what my mom was like when she was 12, or 15, but I have a pretty
good idea of what she was like when she was 17, when she had
me, against everyone's advice. This was in south Dallas, one of the
rougher neighborhoods in Dallas. And everybody said, 'Don't have
that baby, your life will be over.' She said, 'I'm going to have that
baby and we're going to make it.'

She wrote this book, which I thought was great for her, but for
whatever reason I avoided reading the book for a long time. I finally
took it with me when I went on a trip to Mexico, I was by myself
and I said, 'Okay, I'm going to read this book now.' And I'd never
sat down and read a book cover-to-cover (in one sitting). I could not
put it down. It was me, it was my life, it was my mom's life, and it
was about my father, who I don't know, and it was about the other
husband she had, and the description of her poverty, which I never
was really aware of. We were not middle class, we didn't have any
money at all. But I never knew that we were poor, I never knew that
we were struggling.

So I read her book. I cried 50 times, I laughed 30 times. It blew me away. And it came full circle, it's not just a book about when I was two, or ten, it's about when I was 30, as well. It goes through my marriage and my divorce, and what was really her being isolated from my family. It's a complicated story, but the pain that she went through at that time, that's what really tore me up when I was reading, knowing that I had failed her as a son.

The book killed me, it really, really knocked me down. I think it's an amazing book. I was forced to really apologize to her for letting that happen at the time, and it also taught me a lesson as a parent, the way you view your children and how precious they are.

I was the only son, the only child she ever had, and trying to put myself in her shoes when I was sick, what it must have felt like – 'Oh, my god, this is the boy I risked so much to have, and now I might lose him.' I mean, it's just unbelievable. Those five or six hours of reading were really, really heavy.

In your book, *It's Not About the Bike,* you write, "I want to die at 100 years old with an American flag and a star of Texas on my helmet after screaming down an alpine descent on a bicycle going 75 miles an hour. I want to cross one last finish line with my stud wife and 10 children applauding, and I want to lie down in a field of those famous French sunflowers and gracefully expire." How close is that to your dream of the perfect ending?

I don't think I'll even make it to 100 (laugh). But I can't complain. For a 34-year-old guy who grew up as a punk kid in Plano, Texas, I cannot complain. I have my health, I have my happiness, I have three beautiful and healthy children. I have financial security, unbelievable friends, tons of support in the cancer community, and I think I'm at a point now where I can really make a difference.

In racing, if you win you get a yellow jersey. But boy, if you can step in and change the course history when it comes to cancer, that's a big victory.

That and to grasp life for what it is, which you do.

Every day. Every day.

Vijay Singh and Phil Mickelson

Not your cookie-cutter golf gods.

chapter
14

LEFTY & MR. LUNCHBUCKET

You would be hard-pressed to find a more pampered and fawned-upon athlete than the professional golfer. It's an egocentric sport, maybe egomaniacal. If a nuclear bomb was dropped near a tournament, the golfers would complain that the blast created a tough crosswind.

So I'm not going to try to elicit your sympathy for a pair of my favorite athletes who happen to be golfers. But I do want to tell you a little bit about Phil Mickelson and Vijay Singh. I find their stories quietly heroic, and I believe they both have a genuine grasp on reality, an appreciation for the gifts they are blessed with, and they shoot holes in the golfer stereotype.

Both of these men have battled image problems. Mickelson, until he won the 2004 Masters, was labeled a choker. His skills were enormous, but, well, there were questions about Phil's heart.

Singh is saddled with the image of being a joyless workaholic. Some see him as cocky and aloof, even nasty. His remarks in 2004 about Annika Sorenstam competing against the men cemented Vijay's image as the party pooper with the golden swing.

When I approached Singh in 2004 for an interview, I wasn't warmly received. The media has not always been kind to Vijay, or so he feels, and he is wary. But when I told him how much I admired him for what he went through to become the top golfer in the world in 2004, the ice thawed a bit.

This guy's life is like a B movie. Vijay was born in Fiji and as a kid he caddied for a dollar a day at a course near the airport where his father was a mechanic. Very few top golfers – Lee Trevino is the last one I can recall – ever emerged from such a lowly economic background.

One day a pilot gave young Vijay a golf magazine with an article by Tom Weiskopf on how to swing the golf club. That article became Singh's bible, he used it to teach himself to play, and 30 years later he was an overnight PGA sensation.

Singh took the long road to riches, he used all the detours. He dropped out of school at 16 to golf full-time, and he began moving about the globe. He gave golf lessons to lumberjacks in Borneo, he worked as a bar bouncer, he did whatever he had to do to keep golfing.

It's possible that no golfer ever worked as hard at the sport as did Vijay Singh. A couple years ago a sportswriter friend of mine was planning to write a column on Tiger Woods being the hardest working golfer on the tour. And believe me, Tiger does work hard, almost maniacally. But when my friend surveyed other golfers, caddies and golf people as to who is the hardest worker in golf, everyone said the same thing: "You mean besides Vijay?"

I asked Vijay why some people don't like him. He said he has found that many people resent it when a guy like him becomes successful by overcoming obstacles and working hard. At some level they resent your effort and dedication, maybe because it makes them feel like slackers. They tend to rationalize that you win only because you go through life wearing blinders and shunning human contact.

"I'm not here to make friends," Singh admitted. "I come from a country where half of the 850,000 people are Indians whose ancestors came to Fiji as slaves more than a century ago. So we always have a chip on our shoulder, we are always the ones who have much to overcome. I'm not here to have a party. I'm here to do what I need to do, and what I need to do is find a way to win."

Singh was a late bloomer. All of his hard work finally clicked into place about the time he turned 40. It's almost as if Vijay worked so hard that he wore down the golf gods. "The hell with it," they said, "Let the big guy win some tournaments."

In 2004 Singh leapfrogged over Tiger to became the No. 1 ranked golfer in the world. Vijay won nine tournaments and almost $11 million. I was talking to Johnny Miller about Vijay's 2004 season and Miller said, "Sure, Vijay had good timing. Tiger was having an off-year while he worked on a new swing, Phil may have had a letdown after winning the Masters. But what Vijay did in 2004 is the greatest season-long feat since Byron Nelson won 11 events, and in some ways Singh's feat was more difficult. He did all that winning while carrying the unbelievable burden of attention, and of the negative image."

Singh's biggest social blunder was his comment in 2004 that Annika Sorenstam shouldn't be allowed into men's tournaments via sponsor exemptions. Vijay to this day swears that he was both misquoted and misunderstood. He says he was merely expressing a common opinion among PGA players that to give a woman a tournament berth simply for the novelty and publicity value, knocking out a man who had worked long and hard for that berth, is unfair.

"I'm just saying I know what it is to struggle," Singh told me, "and I know what it means for a person to earn that card and earn that spot in the tournament."

This is a man who gets up at 4:30 to run five miles, practice yoga and hit the gym, all before his long golf work day starts.

I found Singh to be interesting, opinionated and thoughtful. He'll never have the gallery appeal of a Fuzzy Zoeller or a John Daly, and that's ironic, because Vijay has worked so hard for his success that he should be the darling of the average joe.

Vijay is simply his father's son – a hard-working mechanic.

* * *

Phil Mickelson is, in some ways, the anti-Vijay. Lefty, as he is called, is one of the most telegenic of all athletes. He's youthful, attractive, has a great smile and seems like a swell guy. The galleries love him. He doesn't have a stone face, he doesn't pull cameras out of the gallery or chastise people who make noise.

He's a big, likeable kid, and that's why so many people were pulling for him when he won the Masters in '04, his first win in a major on his 43rd try.

But the dramatic story of Lefty isn't how he finally won a major, it's how the horror and near-tragedy that he and his family went through made him a much stronger person and – as a residual benefit – a better golfer.

A year before Mickelson won his first Masters, his wife Amy was due with their third child. They have two daughters, Amanda and Sophia, and Evan was to be their first son. The delivery was going smoothly (I know, easy for me to say, I'm a guy) when suddenly Amy's uterus ripped and she began bleeding heavily, a life-threatening situation.

There were no doctors at the hospital with the expertise to stop the bleeding, and not only was Amy's life in danger, but Evan was suffocating. An emergency call went out but the nearest doctor was a 45-minute drive away.

As Amy struggling to stay conscious, Phil was absolutely paralyzed with horror and helplessness. His childhood sweetheart and his infant son were dying before his eyes.

Somehow Amy held on, the doctor arrived and saved both mother and child. Phil was grateful, and he was shaken to the depths of his soul, his life changed forever.

"That night, once I realized my wife was going to live and my child was going to be okay, I vowed that I would never be paralyzed by anything ever again, never allow myself to be so helpless," Mickelson said to me. "I told Amy that because we were given a second chance, we were going to dedicate the rest of our lives to doing everything we can the right way and caring about each other and caring about our children."

Mickelson had never been an ogre, but he became much kinder and more thoughtful to people. He will sign autographs and pose for pictures until he drops. He interacts with the media now in a genuine way, whereas in the past he was sometimes curt and condescending. He and Amy are founding and funding a leadership school.

"After what I went through," Phil told me, "I will never allow myself to brood, to sit around and wonder, 'What if?' I'll just play as hard as I can, every time, because you never know who you're affecting or touching."

Months after his Masters victory in '04, Mickelson received a letter from a woman whose husband died of cancer the Sunday Phil won his first green jacket. The man was a huge Mickelson fan and was near death at the time. Mickelson had a courageous finish that day, birdied No. 17 and sank a 25-foot putt on No. 18 for the win. Just as Mickelson was addressing that last putt, the dying man awoke from a long coma and watched the putt on TV. As Phil stroked the putt, the man closed his eyes and asked his wife, "Did Phil make it?" She said yes and her husband smiled and died.

Mickelson said, "Roy, I can't even tell you what it must be like for people to find strength and to find satisfaction and joy in watching someone like me play a game. I don't want to be presumptuous and think that what I do is important, because it's a game. What that surgeon did with my wife and son, that's important. I will never allow myself to become jaded, because I realize that nothing is owed to me, not even my family."

It used to bother Lefty, privately, when people said he was a choker, he couldn't win the big one. He's way beyond that now. Not because he won that Masters, but because he learned that the big one isn't a golf tournament, it's your life, and the only way you can be a winner is by living fully and with a sense of doing what's right.

I think that's why people are drawn to Mickelson, because they sense that he gets it.

Not long ago I asked Arnold Palmer to name the current player who reminds him most of the young Arnie. And remember, Palmer is close friends with Tiger. Without pausing, Palmer told me, "Phil Mickelson, because he really seems to get a kick out of the game, and the galleries, and he really draws energy from the people and has fun out there. He reminds me of me."

As crazy as it seems, even pro golfers can be real human beings.

chapter 15

FINE WHINES

What bugs me about sports? I tell you what bugs me.

The famous-athlete web sites, I'm no fan of those. That's where the superstar avoids real interaction with the media (and therefore with the fans) by serving up hokum and pabulum, written by some flunky, and sells you the shirts off his back. Visiting one of those websites is as warm and meaningful as a trip to Safeway.

Can we please put an end to high-fiving God after home runs and touchdowns? You know, the hero crosses home plate and points to his Big Hitting Coach in the Sky? Me and You, God!

Is Mr. Slugger is the only person in the ballpark with a direct connection to God at that moment? God's on Slugger's speed-dial? And while blessing Slugger, God obviously is punishing the heathen opposing pitcher or linebacker. It's like God's in a rotisserie league. Hey, it's their fault for not going to chapel this morning. I like Yogi's take: A hitter stepped into the box and made a cross in the dirt with his bat. Yogi stood up, scratched out the cross with his cleats and said, "Why don't you just let Him watch?"

Please, no more reading of prepared statements, usually prepared by an agent or lawyer. One tip-off that it wasn't the player writing that statement is when he uses a phrase like "ipso facto." Try coming home late and reading a prepared statement to your wife or girlfriend.

I'm bleary-eyed from the logo wallpaper that now serves as the backdrop for every press conference. It's the team logo or a sponsor logo repeated 1,000 times, the better to sear the image into your brain.

Have you noticed that there is no longer such thing as a pitching change in baseball? Now it's a Speedy Oil Change Pitching Change, or the Viagra Third-Down Measurement, or the I Can't Believe It's Not Butter Fumble of the Game.

I'm dizzy from the rotating ad signs on the basketball sidelines, and the computer ads on baseball backstops, and now some arenas have video screens that run completely around the arena and flash non-stop commercials. You sit in the arena and you feel like a cockroach trapped inside a pinball machine.

I've had it with the 24-hour sports highlights on TV. We're oversaturated and inundated with scores, information, highlights, commentary on the highlights and highlights of the commentary. I remember fondly the old *Monday Night Football* halftime shows when Howard Cosell narrated the highlights of the previous day's NFL games, a glorious 10 minutes of everything you need to know.

I'm sick of the award shows, especially the ESPYs. They congratulate the athletes, promote the athletes, pay the athletes (in gifts, expenses or other considerations), then claim to be honest and objective news organizations.

I don't want to overanalyze this, but we overanalyze everything. Too many stats, especially in baseball. It's the Billy Beane-ization of sport. I like Billy, he's a very bright and entertaining guy. But enough already about Scott Hatteberg's on-base percentage.

Joe Blow is batting .500 (2-for-4) lifetime against Lefty Johnson. Announcers give us this stat as if it had any meaning, and managers use it to justify strategy. Two-for-four! The two hits were a check-swing dribbler and a feeble pop-up in the sun, but the hitter is hitting .500 so he's King Kong.

I hate college football coaches' TV shows. TV at its worst. Complete fluff and dishonesty. "Sure we're 3-and-11, but I tell you this: every dang one of our starters exhales carbon dioxide, which is a building block of photosynthesis!"

Shock radio shocks me to sleep. Every athletic mistake or failure is blown up to the level of a felony. You didn't boot a ground ball, you fail as a human being and deserve to be attacked by every frantic host and call-in yahoo for your miscue. The "experts" don't question a manager's strategy, they question his manhood, his IQ and his sanity.

I believe this causes fans to become angry and entitled, and promotes the disintegration of relationships between athletes, fans and the media. When did it become so uncool to be cool, to just enjoy the spectacle?

Two all-sports radio stations in Miami were battling for ratings. One station publicly referred to the other as "sissy-boy radio (featuring) a bunch of girlish-type topics." The other station called the first one, "Old, white, nursing-home...fossilized radio." Marconi would be *sooo* proud.

I've had it with the posse. Any posse, and not just those of inner-city basketball players. Finnish lugers have 'em. Some tennis stars travel the world with full-time racket stringers and dog groomers. One basketball player has a buddy on his payroll whose only duty is to wake up the player. A human alarm clock! I wonder, if a guy is rich and famous, is his posse so important that it has a posse?

I'm sick of voodoo economics. TV ratings continue to drop for many sports but broadcast revenues rise. The players make more and more money, the team owners and all the corporate people involved make more and more money, and what's the upshot? Tickets so expensive that you can't attend a live sporting event unless you're Bill Gates. Going to a Lakers game at Staples Center is like checking into the Ritz Carlton.

Sky-high prices drive away the kids. At an NFL game there's nobody under the age of 25. Nobody can afford to take a kid to an NFL game. You can only take your customers, and write it off on your taxes.

While we're fixing things here, can we blow up all the luxury boxes? Sorry – luxury *suites*. Chandeliers, fine art, crystal and silver.

Bulletproof glass to keep out the chill and the annoying crowd noise. Five TV monitors, but nobody's watching the game.

The whole New Elitism of sports is more than annoying. It started in LA. and New York, but it's creeping. Valet parking at a ballgame? Next we'll see moguls carried to their courtside seats on sedan chairs.

I've had it with the $8.50 hot dog. I took my two kids to a ballgame, we got hot dogs, nachos, drinks, and rock-hard "soft" pretzels. Sixty-five bucks for an armload of microwaved synthetic garbage.

And when you buy a ticket, what's that $5 convenience fee? It's not convenient for me to pay an extra $5. It should be called an inconvenience fee.

Extreme tailgating, that loses me. You set up your base camp a week before the game, barbecue a moose carcass and wash it down with a keg of beer, then stagger into the game. It's not a hobby, it's a bizarre lifestyle, we're retrogressing to the caveman days. If it helps you enjoy the game, fine, but please try not to barf up your possumburger on my sneakers, okay?

Is anyone else tired of the shirtless guys with the body paint in the blizzard? One thing this is good for: If any of these guys are ever charged with a crime, they can plead insanity and prove it with a TV clip showing them half naked in a blizzard, waving a barbecued elk leg.

Can we have a new rule that no TV-radio pregame show or postgame show can last longer than the game itself? These shows once provided a pleasant bridge between reality and the event. Now it's paralysis by overanalysis.

I enjoy the Olympics, but I resent being forced into a heavy emotional investment in events I don't care about because they pop onto my TV screen for 10 minutes once every four years, and if I withhold my love, I'm unpatriotic. Ice skating, swimming, volleyball, luge, curling, synchronized anything – lovely sports, all of them, but don't guilt-trip me if I'm not cheering with my heart and soul.

I'm no Communist, but I cringe at the USA! USA! USA! chanting at international events. We know who we are, the other countries know who we are We are the coolest country ever, but let's not rub Nigeria's or Australia's nose in it, okay?

Thank you, I feel much better now.

Mankind and Michael Vick

chapter 16

MANKIND AND MICHAEL VICK

Albert Schweitzer once said, "Until he extends his circle of compassion to all living things, man will not himself find peace."

We've come a long way, but we've got a long way to go before we find peace. Michael Vick showed us that, although news flash: Vick is not the first animal abuser, or even the worst. Mankind has a long, ugly history of cruelty to creatures for fun and profit.

I'm not saying what Vick did wasn't horrible. His crimes made me sick, they were despicable. Nothing can mitigate the ugliness of the gruesome details.

It's ironic, because Vick has always been a symbol of strength, a powerful man playing in our most powerful sport, playing the position that carries the most power. And yet as Seneca the Roman philosopher said, "All cruelty springs from weakness." So Vick becomes the poster boy for weakness.

But he isn't a one-man show. Let's take a step back and look at the big picture.

The ancient Romans staged gladiator fights in the Colisseum, men murdering men for the whooping pleasure of the masses. A favorite feature of those shows was a staggering variety of animal slaughter. Exotic beasts from all over the known world were put to death in as many gruesome ways as the Romans could devise, and they were very creative. Gladiators stalked and killed the animals, or the beasts were forced to fight one another to the death as the crowd howled.

During the California gold-rush, the miners enjoyed staging animal fights, typically a bull verses a grizzly bear, to the death.

We're still at it. Animal abuse for our amusement is widespread, and if we lay all the blame and focus all the outrage on one person, we're missing a big point, and we're guilty of a howling hypocrisy and a blatant double standard.

Look around today.

In Spain and Mexico, bullfighting thrives. The bull is systematically tortured and murdered and a wonderful time is had by all, except the bull.

Defenders of the "sport" say it's deep in the Hispanic culture, and isn't that what we heard about dogfighting? It's part of the rural culture, or the inner-city culture, or whatever. Sure, and slavery was part of the rich culture of the old South.

In England they have foxhunts, which sounds like a ripping good time. And so traditional! It's in the very blue blood of the privileged men who gather 20 or 30 of their pals and a pack of trained dogs, chase a defenseless fox, tree it, kill it for sport (as far as I know they don't barbecue the fox), then ride home celebrating themselves as true sportsmen. Tally ho!

Right here in America, and in Mexico, we have legalized greyhound racing. The dogs are trained using electric prods, and when a dog loses a step, often it is put to sleep. It's done humanely, they say, but isn't this kind of like putting grandpa to sleep when he can no longer mow the lawn?

Then you've got your good old traditional circus. Animal-defense groups make a convincing argument that many circuses train their animals using systematic fear and torture, and those funny and talented creatures live lives of non-stop horror. At best, we're anthropomorphizing the animals, humanizing them by putting a hat on a dog or a suit on a monkey, forcing them to amuse us.

A friend of mine lived across the street from a car dealership that used animals in its advertising. Every year an elephant was brought to the car lot to attract attention. Kids could ride the elephant. My friend found out years later that his son witnessed the elephant keeper stabbing the animal repeatedly with a sharp pole until it would bleed profusely.

And of course, there's good old hunting. Hey, it's cultural. That's how we used to survive, right? But how about the type of hunting where a bunch of yahoos drive their massive off-road vehicle deep into the wilderness, whip out their high-powered, military weapons with telescope sites, blow the brains out of some grazing deer from 150 yards, tie the carcass to the top of the car, and yahoo all the way home?

I'm not saying let's outlaw hunting, especially not when humane methods are used and when the hunters eat what they shoot. But some forms of hunting are cruel and sadistic.

And then there's the cultural sport of dogfighting. It didn't go away when Vick was locked up. The ugly news reports served only to drive the worms deeper underground. The fury will blow over, because we're not as upset about the vast dogfighting "culture" as we are about one famous quarterback's involvement.

Vick really touched a nerve, didn't he? In some ways, he might find it more difficult to blend back into polite society than did O.J. Simpson. But if what Vick did was wrong, ugly, disgusting and worthy of severe punishment, then those of us who condemn him should save some of our anger for animal abuse and cruelty in general.

I just hope we as a society don't say, "Well, they locked up Vick, that takes care of *that* problem."

Because it doesn't, unless we maintain the outrage Vick inspired and use it to make some social progress.

As we rebels liked to say back in the '60s, if you're not part of the solution, you're part of the problem. And it starts with realizing that while Vick is the well-deserving poster dude for animal cruelty, he's just one sick man in an world-wide epidemic.

Vick, an American idiot, opened our eyes. Now let's see if we keep them open.

chapter 17

LOVE NOTES

You cannot make your living in sports, or at least you shouldn't, unless you are a goose-bump guy. Here are some of the things that give me chills and make me glad I lucked into a career that involves great moments, performances, sights and sounds.

So punch up John Coltrane on the jukebox playing "These Are a Few of My Favorite Things."

Wrigley Field, Yankee Stadium, Fenway Park, and the incredible beauty and ambience of Oriole Park at Camden Yards, where the aroma is provided by Boog Powell's barbecue. These ballparks are separate little worlds, and visits to them never fail to get my blood pumping. Put me in one of these temples of baseball with something on the line and I'm a happy man.

Or the stadium in Ann Arbor, Michigan, with 100,000 close friends on a football fall afternoon.

Or the Rose Bowl on New Year's Day, at sunset, the air turning chilly and the last rays of sun dancing with the San Gabriel Mountains. How can it be more beautiful every year?

I love the jolt of electricity running though the crowd before the bell at a heavyweight championship fight. Two giants are about to try to kill one another, and it's all very exciting and very real.

I've never been an auto racing fan, but you stand near the first turn at the Indy 500, the flag drops and here they come, and the sound and power smack you in the chest and knock you backwards.

I love Duke's Cameron Crazies, all passion and noise.

I love the love affair between Brett Favre and the Packers fans. Nothing quite like it. Brett wrote the book on how a great athlete should treat the fans, and the Cheeseheads wrote the book on how to return that love. Nothing phony, nothing held back, a beautiful thing.

Certain voices cut right to the heart. Dave Johnson calling the Kentucky Derby over the PA system at Churchill Downs. "And down the stretch they come!" I don't care if the field is 10 mules and a donkey, you get the chills.

I love to hear Joe Buck calling a ballgame, like an echo of his late father. Jack passed the torch beautifully. Joe is a great announcer, a great guy, and humble. Not a lot of gimmicks, though I like the "Track! Wall! Gone!" Just broadcasting integrity and a commitment to the craft.

Give me Johnny Miller at the mic in a big golf tournament. I've never met anyone so incapable of holding back an honest comment. A gift to golf.

And I know I'm home when I hear Vin Scully invite me (and a million other close friends) to pull up a chair. That's how Vinny has opened his Dodger broadcasts for over 50 years, an invitation to a three-hour poetry reading by Scully.

Derek Jeter, there's something so special about this guy, it's almost spooky. He comes through in the clutch, and he does it in new and crazy ways. Remember the backhand flip to home plate to nail Jeremy Giambi and kill the A's in the playoffs? The swan dive into the stands for that foul ball? A worthy member of the Yankee hall of fame.

There's nothing in sports like Lance Armstrong in the Tour de France, going into the mountains. For the Decade de Lance, the Tour heading into the hills was almost its own season. It's like, Honey, do you remember our first date? Of course I do, it was in '97, the day Lance rode into the mountains.

I love the last out of the Little League World Series, maybe more than the last out of the real World Series. The raw emotion, the joy, the tears. It's life and death with these little guys and I believe they're learning hard and wonderful life lessons.

I loved watching the Red Sox get it done in '04. I'm no rabid Red Sox fan, but I've never seen anything like their run in the playoffs and World Series. It was a remarkable month of real baseball thrills in a magnificent setting.

I love the attitude, style, joy, flair and unworldly skill that a few special people bring to the party: Ozzie Smith's back flip, Emmitt Smith's heart and LeBron James' creativity are three that spring to mind.

For joy, there's Miguel Tejada, who gets more fun out of baseball than the other guys. Miggy reminds me of Magic Johnson.

Some people are put off by Ray Lewis' strutting, but not me. He walks onto the field, he's got his hand up, he's doing that thing with his helmet, and dancing and strutting. It's an exuberance I find endearing and theatrical and real. Sometimes he carries it too far, but at the start, to set the stage, it's like something from the days of the Roman gladiators when the fighters had to impress the fans and intimidate the opponent, or die.

I love watching Kobe Bryant deal. I know he leaves some people cold, but when you try to define the burning need to excel, you just point to Kobe. Arrogant, selfish? No doubt, at times, but still I marvel.

My job would be a bore without the likes of Barry Sanders and Tony Stewart working with a sliver of daylight, or Jim Edmunds outrunning a line drive.

The good in sports always outweighs the bad, by a ton. Put me at any ballgame, any sport, and I'll find something I love and someone I admire. Just give me a game and a hot dog, even an $8.50 hot dog, and I'm a happy guy.

With my sons Andy and Nicky, and Ted Williams

And with Ted, about a year later.

TEDDY BALLGAME

Ted Williams was the last true American hero.

Everything about him was real. No plastic.

If you step back and examine his life, Ted Williams is like a character from a novel, too big to be true. In an age when so much of our culture is blown out of proportion, it's almost impossible to exaggerate Teddy Ballgame.

I met Ted Williams when I was a 21-year-old television rookie in Miami. I interviewed sportswriter John Underwood in Homestead, Florida. Underwood worked for *Sports Illustrated* and he and Williams were long-time buddies, so Williams happened to be there.

Ted was still reasonably young at the time, mid-50ish.

"I know who the hell you are!" he boomed. "You're that kid on the local TV station."

I was flabbergasted. I called him Mr. Williams and he said, "Don't start with that Mr. Williams s#!%! My name's Ted! You call me Ted!"

Thus began my friendship with the most outrageous, profane person I've ever met, and I've been in a lot of locker rooms. Williams was John Wayne with an attitude. Always in charge, always huge, always loud, always the center of attention.

I'm no genius, but I was smart enough to see an opportunity, so I asked Williams if I could interview him on camera.

"I don't do any goddamn interviews!" he bellowed. "But you're the local kid from the local station and you don't know any better."

He did the interview, and it was a huge break for me. I had captured a legend.

I asked him if it was true that his eyesight was so keen that he could see the individual stitches on a baseball pitched to him.

"That's a lot of bunk," he said. "But I'll tell you one thing I could do when I was younger, I could read the label on a jazz record going around the Victrola."

Years later I tried to land Williams again as an interview subject for my TV show, but he was elusive. I must have made 50 tries to reach him and his people and ask – to beg – him to come on the program. No dice.

Then one day in '93 I got a phone call from a man who introduced himself as Buzz Hamon, said he worked for the Ted Williams Museum.

"Ted would like to talk to you," Harmon said.

Then I heard a familiar voice.

"Is this the goddamn kid I spoke to about 20 years ago, who still had fuzz behind the goddamn ears?"

I said, "Hello, Mr. Williams," and he cut me off.

"Don't start with that Mr. Williams s#!%!"

He said, "I need your goddamn body to host an event we're doing in Hernando (Florida), at my museum. I got all kinds of people here but I hear you're a pretty goddamn funny guy, I'd like you to host this thing."

So I flew to Hernando to emcee a fundraising event for Ted's museum. He greeted me, saying, "This is the kid that interviewed me about 20 years ago in Homestead!"

He never forgot anything. His was the brain that catalogued every pitch ever thrown to him, and the details of every at-bat. We did long interview sessions, mostly the two of us walking around his museum, him reminiscing. He got into a lot of personal stuff.

He talked of his third wife, Louise, the true love of his life, and his eyes welled with tears, and this is a man often seen as being devoid of real emotion.

He told stories about his days as a fighter pilot in WWII and Korea.

"We got hit by this goddamn f#!%ing MiG," he said, and he seemed annoyed, or maybe embarrassed because he got shot down. "Whenever I get afraid, I swear something awful. I said, 'If anyone's up there to help me, now's the time!'

"And you know, that goddamn thing was just about ready to go end over end and we had to take that f#!%er down onto the middle of the runway. Well, we hit the runway and one of the tires blew immediately, and I'm hitting the goddamn brakes and we're going about 200, and don't you know, at the end of the runway is about as big a brick wall as you can possibly goddamn find, and I'm trying to stop this goddamn thing because I don't want it tumbling end over end. I'm sticking my leg as hard on the brakes as I can, and the wings are on fire and the cockpit's full of smoke and we're having all kinds of problems.

"You know, I pulled up that goddamn jet about eight feet from that goddamn wall and jumped out just before it blew up! I see fire all around me, I jump out, throw my helmet down and run as hard as I can."

"So after an experience like that," I said, "you probably put in to go home on leave."

"Go *where?*" he said. "I was back in the air the next day!"

As we toured the museum I held onto Ted's arm because his balance was shaky and his vision wasn't good. We'd stop an exhibit and he'd say, "What've we got there, partner?"

I'd say, "Jimmie Foxx," and Ted would say, "Jimmie Foxx! You know, that guy drank 18 ounce-and-a-half miniature bottles of scotch! More than a quart of booze!"

The memories and the stories just poured out, it was like walking through a battlefield with an old soldier. Ted was getting old, and some names and memories blurred. Mark McGwire was at the banquet, and when Williams talked to McGwire he got him confused with Frank Howard, a huge slugger of the '60s. Williams spoke to McGwire as if he were Howard, explaining how Ted's teams used to pitch to Howard.

Some other things Ted said:

- "As a kid, internally I was a little scared of how I might do (in the big leagues). Or not do. I never had quite the guidance at 16, 20. Life magazine wanted to do a story on me when I was 19, I said no."
- "Did I have as much fun as I should have? No, I don't think I did. I wrote a book and the guy asked me, 'Tell me some funny things that happened.' I had an awful hard time thinking of even a couple."
- "What did I love about hitting, specifically? I've always thought that the sound of the bat on a real good rippy ball sounded awfully good."
- "Joe (DiMaggio) was a much better player than I was. I'd watch him. The way he ran, way he hustled, his quickness at the plate. Better hitter? No, I don't think he was."

At one point Ted asked me, "What's the name of that little black guy down in San Diego, my home town, who has that pea-shooter of a bat?"

He meant Tony Gwynn, and they happened to be very warm friends, Ted's memory for names notwithstanding. Williams called everybody Kid or Fella.

"Yeah, Tony Gwynn, with that little pea shooter! He oughtta be goddamn ashamed of himself, taking that thing up to the plate."

Ted and Tony were soul brothers, they had in common a life mission of mastering the mysterious art and science of hitting a baseball. To Williams, hitting a ball was almost the very meaning of life, and once his career was over, he devoted much of his life to passing the torch, sharing his great secrets with the select few hitters who could comprehend what Ted was teaching and could actually put the lessons to use.

At no time was Ted's life so meaningful as when he was able to connect on a psychic level with a young hitter, although Gwynn frustrated him a bit.

"He disappointed me slightly when he says, 'I don't guess (at pitches),'" Ted said. "Why not guess the first pitch? Why not guess the second pitch? Why not guess the third pitch?"

But no question, Gwynn was a rapt student of Teddy Ballgame. Tony once explained to me the strange way Williams passed the torch to him. And you have to understand that Tony Gwynn was one of baseball's all-time most dedicated students of hitting.

"The first time I met Ted Williams," Gwynn told me, "he said, 'Major league history is made on the ball inside,' And I went, 'On the ball inside?' And he said, 'On the ball inside.' And I kind of stood there waiting for him to explain it a little bit more and he never did. He never did.

"And so you take that statement and if you're a hitter and you're willing to pay the price, it's like trying to figure out a math problem, you try to figure out what he's talking about. You go to the cage. You take batting practice and when they come inside you work on trying to handle the ball. It takes a while to figure it out if they don't give you the answer, and Ted didn't give me the answer, so I was left to my own devices.

"I basically kind of went back to school. I'd hit every day, hit off the tee, look at video, I'm trying to figure out what he meant. Well, it took me two years, and I figured it out one day in Oakland. I hit a home run straightaway and it dawned on me what he was talking about. It's kind of a two-fold answer. The first part of it is, if somebody comes inside and you hit the ball out of the ballpark, guess what, they don't come inside any more. The second thing is, you face these pitchers a lot, it's not like college or high school where you face a guy one time. You face the same guys year in and year out.

"So in facing those guys, you kind of get a feel for how they're going to pitch to you, how they're going to attack you. And in those situations, instead of being defensive, you've gotta be offensive. You've got to be more aggressive.

"It was like the light bulb went on and I said, 'Well, I think what he's saying is that I need to be more aggressive, I need to attack instead of being defensive. Because the first 12 years I can honestly say I was more a defensive hitter, a counter-puncher, where the last eight or nine years I got a little bit more aggressive, I tried to make some things happen. And for the most part I thought I was a much better hitter at the end of my career."

After retiring from the Padres, Gwynn became a college baseball coach. And so the mysterious lessons of the master, Theodore Williams, are being passed along to a new generation of kids who barely know who Ted Williams is, yet his soul is in their swing.

When I last met with Ted, he was near the end of his long life, decades removed from baseball greatness, but it was as he had never left the game. Here's a story he related to me:

"When I was sick and had my second stroke, lying in bed and I was low, so low, ready to give it all up, and I had a dream that I was in spring training with the Red Sox. And Randy Johnson was getting ready to pitch for the other team. Now, the kids on the (Boston) team, I'm there helping them learn how to hit, and the guys start kidding me, 'Go up and take a couple cuts, go up and just look at him.'

"So I kept hearing that and I said, 'All right, I'll go up there and look at him.' The first ball was a whistler, and I said, 'Boy, this guy's got it.' I said to myself, 'I'm not gonna try to pull this guy.' The next thing I said was, 'I'm gonna make him throw strikes.' I saw that one pitch, it didn't cost me anything, now I knew how fast he was, so then I said, 'I'm gonna try to hit him through the box.' The next pitch was a beauty and I just pushed at it, base hit through the middle.

"All the guy says is, 'Boy, what a hitter. What a hitter.'"

That he was.

With Bobby Knight

Just before he turned on me.

chapter 19

A GOOD KNIGHT
A BAD KNIGHT

As my crew is setting up on the gym floor for my interview with Bobby Knight, I chat briefly with one of Knight's team managers, a student in a motorized wheelchair. He is severely challenged, with cerebral palsy. Our conversation is interrupted by Knight Himself, returning from a meeting.

"You sunuvabitch, goddamn, what have you been doing?"

Knight is screaming at the kid, and the harangue lasts maybe a minute. The kid says nothing, kind of smiles. Finally the red-faced Knight turns and leaves. My crew and I are frozen in horror, jaws agape.

A couple of us walk up to the kid, tell him how sorry we are about what just happened. Poor kid must be traumatized for life.

"Why be sorry?" he asks, unruffled.

"Because Knight just humiliated you."

"That's the way coach always talks to me," he says. "See, the last thing I want is for people to talk down to me, pity me or treat me like I'm different. When coach swears at me, I'm a part of the team. I'm a normal guy."

Knight has left us stunned and confused. As I would discover, that's the way you spend most of your time around Bobby Knight.

Did Knight rail at this kid in the wheelchair because of the coach's extraordinary compassion and insight into the human condition? Or is Knight simply an equal-opportunity horse's ass? Genius or tyrant? You tell me. I don't know.

Knight slips into and out of absolute labels like Houdini got out of ropes. I do know that Bobby is a teacher, and he taught me more than I ever learned from any other interview subject. He taught me the hardest lesson I ever learned in the business, a lesson that momentarily cost me my reputation and almost my job; gave me my darkest day in my working life, but made me stronger and smarter.

The first lesson I learned from Knight: Approach with caution and be prepared for anything.

I had made several calls to Knight's office at Indiana, leaving messages, hoping he would agree to an interview. I was fascinated with the character, the many images of Knight. I knew he wasn't a one-dimensional whacko. John Feinstein, who wrote *A Season on the Brink*, told me Knight is the worst person he has ever known, and one of the best.

I criticized Knight on the air on occasion for his various crazed misdeeds. His standard reaction to media criticism is, "This person has never met me, doesn't know me, how can he or she possibly criticize me?" I didn't buy that. I never met Abe Lincoln but I feel justified in forming opinions about him.

Anyway, Knight was fresh off one of his national-debate-stirring Bobby Moments, and I wanted to get the guy into the chair for a prime-time extended interview.

So I'm in Miami for Superbowl XXXIII, and the phone rings.

"Mr. Firestone? Please hold for Bob Knight."

Remember, we've never met, never spoken.

"What the f#*% do you want to talk to me for?" is Knight's hello. "You don't f#*%ing know me, you rip me, you got a lot of flicking nerve to ever write a word about me."

Even over the phone he is scary, angry and vicious. I sense that groveling will not be a wise strategy.

"Who the f#*% are you to talk to me like this?" I ask. "You don't know me, either, and you start blasting me with f-words, acting rude. If you don't want to do an interview, why'd you call me back?"

There is a brief silence, then Knight says, "When do you want to do this?"

He has knocked me off-stride again.

"An interview?" I say.

"Yeah."

"You serious?"

"I've got a couple slow weeks coming up," he says in a stern, slow voice. "You could come down, I could set you straight, because you don't know your ass from your elbow."

"Fine," I say. "By the way, does that one sweater you own still fit you?"

We go back and forth, now bantering like old buddies. He has switched instantly from terrifying hostility to genial jocularity. Was his opening a test? Does he shift real moods that quickly? If Knight's intent is to keep people off-balance, he has mastered the art.

I arrive at Bloomington for the first interview, I'm waiting for Knight in his office and I put my jacket down on his chair. My back is turned to the door and I hear the bear roar.

"Who the f#*% left this f#*%ing jacket on my f#*%ing chair?"

I turn and he breaks into a huge smile, "Oh, Roy Firestone! What a great honor to meet you."

So now we're buddies, right? Who knows?

The interview goes so-so, at first. He's answering everything in detail, almost too long-winded, a lot of blah-blah boilerplate stuff. We're getting bogged down in small talk, it's a Bobby filibuster.

Then I bring up the name Connie Chung, and boom, we're off to the races.

"Let me tell you something about Connie Chung. She's a total fraud, a charlatan, a manipulator."

To refresh: In a taped interview with Chung a year or so earlier, during what Knight thought was a break in the filming, he tossed off his infamous line about rape: "If it's inevitable, sit back and enjoy it."

Knight asked Chung to please not use that comment in the final edit of the interview. She assured him that it would be cut. But it wasn't, it was played to the world. Knight was publicly flayed for weeks. He felt ridiculed, humiliated and betrayed.

Now, facing me, he rips into Chung, then expands his attack to the American media. This guy's a fraud, that guy's a jerk. Rick Reilly is an ass, so is Feinstein. Now it feels like we're getting bogged down again, so I change the subject.

"Bob, how would you have reacted if you found out your son was gay?"

He looks up, then says, "You have to understand, I'm from a different time. But I love my boys, and the first thing I would do is try to get him some rehabilitation, like a drug addict."

I'm thinking, this is unbelievable. I know Knight means to sound compassionate, and I feel like Ted Koppel in the Al Campanis interview, hoping the subject will somehow dig himself out of the hole.

But unlike Koppel with Campanis, we're not live. So later on, I get to make a judgment call. Normally we work "live tape," we run the interviews pure and unedited. But editing is always an option.

I discuss it with my producer. Should we run this? Really, is this relevant?

I have a problem with how some people in our industry manufacture controversy, allowing something relatively small to overwhelm the bigger story. I'm not trying to protect Knight so much as I want to prevent a possibly-misstated sentiment from overwhelming and distorting the interview. If I leave it in, Knight could say, "I do a two-hour interview, and *this is all anybody notices?*"

It's my show, it's my call. I decide to edit out the comment. It would have made a great sound-bite teaser for promos, but it would be exploitative. In effect, I bail Knight out. Remember this, because you'll see how he decided not to return the favor.

Next I ask Knight about Woody Hayes, the controversial ex Ohio State football coach. There are amazing parallels between

Hayes and one of his greatest admirers, Knight. Both are volatile personalities, both great coaches. Hayes' career ended when he punched an opposing player. Knight's career has almost ended more than once due to similar bizarre eruptions.

I ask Knight if he sees any parallels, good or bad, between himself and Hayes.

"Let me tell you," Knight says, "when Woody Hayes hit that guy at the Gator Bowl and lost his job, I sat down and cried like a baby. I picked up the phone, there was this guy Bill Flemming who did football for ABC, I tried to get him to do an interview with Hayes, get Hayes to say he was sorry for what he did. Had Woody done that, he would have been able to finish his career with dignity.

"I tried to set up the interview. 'Coach Hayes, just say you're sorry.' Roy, you know, I couldn't get Woody Hayes to admit he'd done something wrong. That was real disappointing. He wrote a letter to Charles Bauman (the student Hayes punched), but he couldn't bring himself to go public, say, 'I screwed up. I'm human. I'm sorry.'"

Here's my opening. Recently, a film clip has run repeatedly on TV of a practice incident where Knight chokes one of his players.

"You say you wanted Woody to say he's sorry. Tonight, Bobby Knight, can you, whether you think this whole thing is fair or not, can you simply say 'I'm sorry'?"

Knight couldn't do it. And he didn't see the irony.

Well, we aren't making interview history, but I'm really starting to like this guy. He's smart as hell, has a tremendous amount of compassion. When one of his players, Landon Turner, was paralyzed, Knight helped Turner graduate, helped pay the medical bills out of speaking fees, and helped Turner be symbolically drafted by the NBA. Bobby broke down and cried when that took place.

Knight tells me about his son, Pat, whom Bob kicked off the team for a drinking incident, and he tells how they forged a bond. In Pat's last year, on Senior Day, Bobby introduced his team, said, "I've had many great players here. Let me introduce you to my favorite player," and the world's toughest, meanest man broke down and cried.

Knight has a rock-hard set of values. He's not a fan of John Wooden because Knight believes Wooden portrayed himself as a Mr. Chips, saintly guy, while letting UCLA booster Sam Gilbert do the dirty work.

Knight won't break a rule and won't allow anyone else to break one, and if they do, he'll punish them by breaking every known rule of behavior and propriety.

I hang around Knight for a week, with total access to him and his team. He takes me to lunch, shows me around campus like I'm a blue-chip recruit.

He takes me hunting, which isn't my thing. I'm a Jew from Miami Beach. He fires his gun about a foot from my ear. I think he's trying to startle me, and he does.

I ask Knight what's the biggest animal he ever shot. A deer? He's horrified. Why would I think he would shoot a deer? He could never kill a beautiful animal like that.

We talk ball. He says he loves Dennis Rodman's game, would love to have a guy like that on his team. He's not crazy about Michael Jordan's jewelry, but if a guy plays like that, he can wear a dress.

He says he could never coach in the NBA – too little chance to actually teach and coach. There's another Knight irony for you. To an extent, his behavior got in the way of his teaching and coaching. He's all about being straight, not making yourself the center of attention, being in absolute control. Then he goes bonkers and chokes his own player.

Knight continually fails to practice what he preaches, and it's sad that he can't see that. He responds angrily to all criticism, unless it's from his wife. She'll calm him down by saying, "Bob, the horse is dead 20 minutes now. Get off the horse." And like a little kid, he calms down. "You're right," he says to her.

Capturing Knight in a neat box for the viewing audience, I'm learning, is going to be next to impossible. And I'm in a spot. If a majority of viewers view Knight as an idiot or lunatic and I tell them what a swell person he is, I will be branded a suck-up and kiss-ass. On the other hand, if I say that he is villainous and mean-spirited, an angry man who chokes kids and intimidates cripples, I'm not presenting the whole picture.

Now we come to the second part of our two-part TV interview, and it's time for old Roy to take his journalistic swam dive into an empty pool.

We're going to talk about the Neil Reed choking incident, and this will be the first time Knight has discussed it in an interview.

I have not seen the tape. Sounds crazy, because I pay close attention to everything that goes on in sports, and I do my interview homework. But somehow, this one fell into a crack. The snippet of film was shown on TV a million times, but I always missed it. No big deal, right? Everyone knew what was on the tape.

The program format calls for Digger Phelps and I to interview Knight live. I do the first half of the show one-on-one with Knight, then Digger does 15 minutes with him, then I'd wrap it up. Among the topics: Neal Reed, and Indiana's "zero tolerance" directive to Knight.

Unbeknownst to me, Digger has made a promise to Knight that we will not show the choking tape. Digger doesn't tell anyone else about the deal – not the producer, the guys in the truck, me, nobody. When we chatted earlier, I had mentioned to Digger that I hadn't seen the tape, but that I'd roll it during the interview and have Knight explain and comment. Even then, Digger didn't tell me about his deal with Knight.

I'm ready for the interview, seven minutes to air time, the Indiana sports information director walks onto the set, notices the monitor with a freeze-frame of the Neal Reed choking, says, "You're not running that."

What?

"Coach Knight is not doing the interview if you show this tape."

So Knight has his deal with Digger, and Digger has told him that I never saw the clip. The interview has become a poker game and Knight has a fist-full of aces.

Steve Anderson, vice president of ESPN, rushes in, asks what's the problem? The clock is ticking, now Anderson and Digger get into it, screaming at each other. With seconds to go before the opening cue, Knight saunters onto the set, puts on his mike.

During the early going we talk about accepting blame and Knight says, "Ducking has never been one of my characteristics."

There's my opening and I say, "All right, I know we're not gonna duck the Neal Reed incident. We've all seen the tape, although you haven't seen the tape."

Knight:

Have you?

Firestone:

I have not actually seen the tape, ironically enough...But my question to you is, based on what everyone else has seen, what is your view of that incident and what was going through your mind in the midst of all of that?

Knight:

In the midst of the tape being played, or...?

Now he's messing with me.

Firestone:

No, in the midst of at least grabbing Neal Reed. You have to acknowledge you did grab Neal Reed.

Knight:

Well, my take on the whole thing, Roy, is this. You take all of the negotiations that were made prior to that tape being shown. And then you take exactly what took place on that tape and you compare the allegations to what you see on the tape and then you or anyone else can simply draw their own conclusion.

Firestone:

Not to put you on the spot, but why wouldn't you look at the tape?

Knight:

I didn't need to look at the tape to know that I hadn't choked anybody, 'cause I've never choked anyone. So I didn't need to look at the tape for that.

A tap-dancer supreme. Knight could let me off the hook, as I did to him in the earlier interview, but he is now taking great pleasure in turning the tables on the media. He's got me, and he is almost gleeful.

Near the end of our time the producer is telling me in my earpiece, "The switchboards are lighting up. You've got to get him to look at the tape."

So I give it a shot. "If you're so confident about how you approached Neal Reed, why wouldn't you look at the tape? If you're confident about how you felt about it, don't you want to see it?"

"No, not really, I don't need to see it. I looked at the tape, Roy, probably twice after practice was over and so I've seen the tape and that's three years ago."

"So you're comfortable with the way that sits."

"I don't need to look at it."

When Bobby got into coaching, the world lost a great trial attorney. He had me and he knew it.

Months later I would ask the sports information director why Bobby did that to me after I had helped him. "That's Bob," he said. "He had to twist the knife. He could have let you go, but it was an easy way for him to get back at the media."

I had seen Knight's genuine compassion, experienced his seemingly genuine back-slapping, I now I had seen the dark Knight.

The day after the interview, I am a pig roasting on a spit. I didn't run the clip, and I admitted not having seen it. I get 300 phone calls – newspaper, radio and TV people asking, "You call yourself a journalist?"

Funny, but overall the interview went well. Digger and I both asked Knight tough questions. For instance, I said to Knight, "Toughness and discipline, Bob, is not the same thing as bullying and abusiveness. They're not extensions of one another. Do you think you or your supporters have confused the two?"

I asked him if he was happy with his anger management over the last 12 years, and if he thought he needed professional help.

Overall, I felt we gave the world a glimpse into the heart and soul of the man, gave the viewers a real interview.

But the substance of the interview was buried in the rush to string me up for not having seen the tape and thus giving Knight a way to wriggle off the hook.

All anyone wanted to talk about was Roy's boo-boo, going on-air without having seen the strangulation tape. And speaking of ducking, I knew that wasn't an option, so I did as many interviews as I could.

It was painful. The more interviews I did, the more I wasn't sure if my crime was failing to watch a videotape, or axe-murdering a family of six. And remember, at this point I'm still unaware of the deal Digger had made with Knight.

Funny thing: I asked several of my interrogators, "Did you see the interview?" About 70 percent of them said no. I asked them, "Do you see the irony here? You're ripping me for not seeing the clip, but you didn't see the clip of me not seeing the clip."

Still, I have goofed, and this was easily the low point of my career. It helped when I talk to Rick Reilly and he said, "You know what, Roy? It's your turn. I've taken it. Jim Gray has taken it. It's your turn. I hear you did a great interview, but some people, all they want to do is take something that is meaningless and use it for fodder. You asked him about the choking, didn't you? OK, then, what's the big deal? This isn't about you."

I learned. If you're in my business long enough, you're going to take a fall or two. For a week, I knew what it must be like to be Bobby Knight and feel the unfair (or so it seemed) wrath, experience the media feeding frenzy, the distortion of priorities, the loneliness.

It was a great lesson for me, in trust and preparation, in awareness and the power of the media. I learned from a master.

With Magic Johnson

The awesome power of a smile.

I BELIEVE IN MAGIC

Here's what I have learned from Earvin "Magic" Johnson: Believe.

When Magic boarded the Los Angeles Lakers' flight to Philadelphia for Game 6 of the 1980 NBA Finals, he told the handful of reporters on board that his coach had just told him he would be playing center the next night, in place of injured team captain Kareem Abdul-Jabbar.

Center? A rookie point guard playing center in a huge game, in place of the man who would be voted that season's NBA MVP?

Magic was so unruffled that the reporters assumed he was either acting cool to avoid panic, or he was in denial. Or in shock. Play center?

"Oh, I know I can do it," Johnson said. "I played center in high school.'

"So did I, Magic," said a 6-foot-2 reporter.

Magic smiled.

The next night, playing center – and guard, and forward – Johnson scored 42 points and grabbed 17 rebounds as the Lakers won the NBA Championship.

Fast-forward to 1991, Earvin Johnson is announcing to a stunned world that he has tested positive for HIV. He would be leaving the Lakers, of course. Someone at the press conference asked, "Where will you go?"

"I'm not goin' anywhere," Magic said.

And he didn't. He stayed and fought.

I learned, and I believe. Magic Johnson is a man of his word.

Magic is a spokesman for all sorts of businesses and products and causes, but I don't look at him as a spokesman for anything. To me he is an extraordinary symbol of possibility.

Since receiving his death sentence and "retiring," Earvin has won an Olympic gold medal, won an All-Star Game MVP award, coached the Lakers, been part-owner of the Lakers, hosted a TV talk show, barnstormed the world with his own basketball team, sparked an economic revival in the inner cities as builder and owner of several businesses, raised a family and promoted awareness of AIDS.

When we did an interview in '97 Magic told me, "We need to educate people, but that said, the whole idea of this being a death sentence has changed. You look around, see people (with AIDS and HIV) living quality productive lives. I've had the time of my life. I've never had more fun, never had more ambition and excitement in everything I do."

It wasn't easy, though. Always, behind the amazing, "effortless" success of Magic, has been hard work and pain. He talked then about how devastating it had been back in '91.

"People were whispering when I would come into a room, and when I'd get a little bit closer, they wouldn't even whisper, they'd just stop talking."

I asked if that made him sad.

"Not really, Roy. But it was hard to believe people couldn't just come up to me. The first couple of months, people didn't know if they should hug me or kiss me or stay away, or be in another room, or talk to me through a window."

I mentioned Karl Malone's famous statement about being afraid to be on the court with Magic, and he laughed.

"Yeah, Karl Malone says a lot of dumb things. Listen, I'm not an I-told-you-so person, but the proof is there. It's 12 years later, here I am. I'm not gloating, but God has made me, I think, a symbol – not for AIDS or HIV or anything, but for having a positive attitude.

"I think I made AIDS blink. I don't think I made it go away, but I think I made it blink. I also think I made it open its eyes wide. Now maybe we can talk about it more openly. Now maybe we don't have to whisper. Because of people who have dealt with it, like Arthur Ashe and Greg Louganis and myself, we have an awareness we didn't have in '91. But the main thing we don't have is a fear, a fear that eats you up. Roy, I'm in a high school the other day and they got questions! These are questions people were afraid to ask in '91."

Magic talked about a TV show he taped for Nickelodeon shortly after his diagnosis. Linda Ellerbee was the host and they were talking with school kids about AIDS. There was a nine-year-old girl named Wysteria who had HIV. He asked her what it was she wanted people to understand, and she burst into tears.

Telling me the story, Magic became emotional.

"I was still embracing that girl when we went to commercial, and everybody was crying – her, me, Linda Ellerbee, the camera crew. And that was the time I finally let go of my own emotions, I said to myself at that moment, this has got to be my priority."

"Is it a burden?" I asked.

"Of course it's a burden. Funny thing is, as tough a burden as it is, people think I don't carry burdens because I try to keep a positive attitude, and that makes it tougher. And you look at the things I've done, but some people think I should do more."

I mentioned that he had sparked a business revival in Baldwin Hills, an area of L.A. where black-owned businesses thrived until almost all were burned down or wiped out in the Rodney King riots.

"It's funny you say that, Roy," Magic said, "because I look at that as a symbol, too. My life was almost burned to the ground, my career was certainly burned to the ground. They took me from basketball, then somebody, maybe God, said, 'I've got a bigger plan for you.'

"So what do we need to do? *We need to rebuild your career.* So I tried coaching. And the Olympic team. *We need to build your interests.* I tried a talk show. People criticize me for that, say I was looking for the spotlight, but the truth is, I was just doing all the things I always dreamed of doing. When I was a kid I dreamed of having my own talk show. All the things I did I dreamed about, so how can they tell me I shouldn't try to live those dreams?"

Some of Magic's dream-chasing led to frustration. As a coach, he had trouble dealing with a generation of less-dedicated-than-Magic players. At one Lakers practice, center Vlade Divac's pager beeped and Magic snatched it and hurled it against a wall, smashing it to pieces. Magic's talk show was widely panned.

"What AIDS taught me," he said, "was to love your dreams more. The biggest thing I dreamed when I was a kid," and here Magic began to cry, "I always wanted to be treated as more than just a ballplayer. I wanted to be viewed as a businessman, someone who could see something and make it happen. So when I talked about rebuilding inner cities, and people told me there was no money there and nobody to do it, I said we had to do it, we need to put some pride in this community."

And he did it. He built theaters, and Starbucks stores, TGIFriday restaurants, Fatburger stands, 24-Hour Fitness centers. All of them are built in inner-city areas where it was impossible to get financing, and impossible to sustain growth because of the low economic level of the area. But Magic Johnson made it happen, and his businesses employ thousands of kids, mostly neighborhood African Americans who, until Magic came along, had to take long bus rides to even apply for legitimate jobs.

Magic is proud of what he has done, but he's prouder of what the kids and the people of the neighborhoods have done with the opportunities he provided them.

He said, "You can't just talk the talk, 'Get an education,' and everything will be fine. You have to walk the walk. You gotta show them by opening opportunities. Then they get it because they see it. They see I'm real. I don't drive up in a limo. I touch them, I hug them, I tell them I came from a family of 10 and we were poorer than poor."

He makes them believe.

"You know the thing we don't have in our (inner city) community?" he said. "We don't have quality services, and that's one of the things I'm proudest of. In Atlanta a woman came up to me and said, 'Magic, I've lived in this community 40 years and I couldn't get a salad within a five-mile drive of my house. Now I have this restaurant. God's gonna keep you for this.'"

He started to get choked up again.

"I know those basketball things were great, the things we all did, but that's just basketball. What we're doin' here is going to mean something."

Now the tears were flowing.

"You have to go back to be happy. I'm crying for joy, because I had this dream for so many years, and now it's a reality."

The assist, that's what Magic is all about. Wherever he goes, he's dishing off to open teammates. When he was diagnosed, I quoted a line from a Jackson Browne song, "Fountain of Sorrow."

You could be laughing at me, you've got the right
But you just keep on smiling, so clear and so bright.

Magic could be laughing at us, but not an ounce of cynicism or bitterness has crept into his soul.

For our interview, we sat in one of his theaters and projected photo images from his life on the giant screen. First, Magic at about nine, dribbling.

"There you are," I said, "playing by yourself."

"Oh, I always played by myself. I was Wilt Chamberlain of the Philadelphia Warriors on one side, and Dave Bing of the Detroit Pistons on the other side. And I would do the radio play-by-play. 'Wally Walker to Hal Greer, Greer passes off to the Dipper, slaaaaaam dunk!'"

Then a snapshot of Magic at Everett High in East Lansing, him with a gigantic afro. Then at Michigan State.

"Look," he said, "it's '79, there's that blond-haired kid, Larry Bird. His team (Indiana State) has won 33 in a row, the stage is set. They had beat DePaul, we beat Penn, here we are for the NCAA championship. They cut our lead to five, and I drove the ball down the lane and dunked it, and we won.

"I saw Larry Bird crying, I saw a towel over his head, and I felt like telling him, 'I'm sorry you lost, but my only real sorrow is that this game has to end.'".

On the screen, a clip of the last play of Magic's first NBA game. Kareem hits a sky hook to beat the Clippers and Magic jumps into Kareem's arms at mid-court, hugs him and won't let go.

"Kareem is saying, 'Kid, we've got 81 more of these, you gotta lighten up.' And I'm saying, 'Big Fella, if you keep doing it like this, I'm gonna keep hugging you and you ain't gonna get rid of me.'"

That's Magic. He keeps hugging life. It can try to push him away, but he just hangs on and hugs harder. His passion is absolutely startling.

We ran a clip Magic's hook shot, his "junior-junior-junior skyhook" that won Game 4 of the 1987 NBA Finals against the Celtics.

"I'm just sorry this movie ever ends," he said.

"It hasn't ended," I said.

"No," he said, "this is just the preview of coming attractions."

With Paul McCartney and Elton John

Sometimes your dreams come true.

ROCKSTARS & SHORTSTOPS

I deal with sports celebrities on a daily basis, and while I like many of them and admire what they do, I left the hero-worship stage behind several decades ago.

With rock stars, it's a different story, and I'll tell you about a couple of guys I've met where you could say I've been star-struck.

I am a serious Beatles fan and a collector of their memorabilia. Like a zillion other people, my life has been greatly touched by the Beatles.

In 1999, Paul McCartney was at the Los Angeles House of Blues to promote *Run, Devil, Run*. It was an event for record execs, but I wrangled an invitation from a friend, and I met Paul, very briefly.

I also met his personal-affairs manager, Bill Porricelli, a former walk-on football player at Penn State. Paul isn't a big sports fan but Porricelli is, and we hit it off and became good friends.

A month later I read that Paul was planning to celebrate the 40th anniversary of the Beatles breakthrough at the Cavern Club in Liverpool, by playing a one-night gig there.

I knew it was crazy, but I decided I had to go. I phoned Porricelli, told him I had to go. He said he could get me in. A week later I'm flying to England. Bill has set everything up, even alerting the media that a "major American journalist" (his phrase, not mine) is flying in for the concert. I'm met at the airport by newspaper and TV crews, like I'm a Beatle.

I brought a friend along a friend name Mike, and some of McCartney's people pick us up at the airport and give us the grand tour of Paul's town. We see his old home, his high school, Penny Lane, Strawberry Fields where John grew up. We visit the graveyard where Father John McKenzie is buried next to Eleanor Rigby. You talk about getting goosebumps.

The concert was incredible. There were about 80 people crammed in this hot, sweaty underground club where the Beatles got their start, and I was about five feet away from Paul and his band.

Mike and I had backstage passes, but it was a madhouse so we didn't see Paul. But as we were leaving the club, a nice security guy told me, "There is a private reception just around the corner for Paul's people. I'm sure it would be fine for you to go."

We went to the place, a little restaurant, again packed people. We meet Paul's brother and some of Paul's old high school chums. Paul was nowhere in sight. I didn't really expect to get to talk with him, so about two in the morning I said to Mike, "I don't think Paul's going to show. It's been fun, but let's take off."

I saw Mike's eyes look over my shoulder, and it was as if he had just spotted Bigfoot.

"What?" I said.

Mike whispered, "He's...right...behind...you."

I turned around and there was Paul, standing by himself a few feet away, just taking in the scene. He saw me and got a quizzical look on his face. He pointed at me. He stood there for a long moment, staring and pointing.

I was speechless. Why was he pointing at me? There's no way he would remember our brief meeting at the House of Blues. We're both speechless. It's a standoff. The rocker and the gawker.

Then, over Paul's shoulder I saw one of his PR people looking at me, and she tried to help me out. She gave me the pantomime camera-roll hand sign for "movie." I still didn't get it, and Paul was still staring and pointing, and the woman finally mouthed the words, "The movie. The movie. *Jerry Maguire.*"

I said to Paul, "Do you know me from *Jerry Maguire?*"

Paul's music is in that movie, and he must have watched the film dozens of times to make sure his music was properly placed, so he's seen my little cameo role.

His eyes get wide and he said, "Okay! All right! 'You don't want to make me cry, Roy. Don't make me cry.'"

Paul was impersonating Rod Tidwell being interviewed by Roy Firestone. For one brief, surrealistic moment, I was a movie star being saluted by Paul McCartney.

For this bit-part Hollywood actor, folks, that moment was a career highlight.

A postscript: In the wake of 9/11, McCartney became a big Yankee fan. He has lived in New York for 25 years and he was moved by the way the Yankees rallied behind the city, and vice versa. It reminded him of his boyhood in Liverpool, where his dad was a volunteer fireman, and the community was united behind its soccer team.

Paul started going to games and took to wearing a Yankee cap while strolling about town. Porricelli wanted to introduce Paul to Yankee centerfielder Bernie Williams, who learned classical guitar while growing up in Puerto Rico. Bill asked me how to make the intro and I told him to simply take Paul into the Yankee clubhouse.

Porricelli did, and Bernie Williams, a shy and quiet guy, went berserk. He rushed across the clubhouse and put a bear hug on Paul, for about two minutes.

Bernie told Paul, "You don't know how much you have inspired my music. I would give anything if you would only listen to my tape."

McCartney took Bernie's tape, listened, and told Porricelli, "We've got to do something with this guy."

Paul agreed to manage Bernie and publish his music, then he rounded up several famous musicians to record with Williams. Bernie's first album shot to No. 3 on the American jazz charts.

Paul was no frustrated jock, but I do believe that Elton John, if he could, would trade his music career for a chance to be a utility infielder for the Atlanta Braves.

I got a big surprise when I met Elton, also in '99. I was in Las Vegas to emcee Andre Agassi's annual charity fundraiser, and as part of an upcoming ESPN show on Andre, I was gathering sound bites from celebrities in town for the gala. I thought it would be fun to get Elton John, because he's a huge Agassi fan, and because he's Elton John.

However, people kept telling me that Elton doesn't do interviews. I decided to take a shot anyway, if I could dream up a way to approach him. I didn't have to. He approached me.

During an afternoon press conference where several of the stars were milling about, Elton pointed to me (what is it with these rock stars pointing to old Roy?) and said, "Hey, how are you doing?"

How did he know me? I had no idea. We chatted for a minute and before I had a chance to ask him about doing an interview, he said, "We must sit down and do an interview."

We set it up, we got together in his dressing room and he launched in with great enthusiasm.

"I must tell you, Roy," he said, "I've got to be the biggest Atlanta Braves fan in the world."

Elton said his love for the Braves started in the mid 1960s when he was a young rock phenom touring America and would find himself trapped in his hotel rooms. He tired of watching the soaps and got into watching baseball because, as he said, it's a soap opera with real people.

The Braves were lousy back then, but they were easy to follow because so many hotels were hooked up to the Braves Superstation, so they became Elton's team. He has his people arrange satellite hookups at every tour stop, and his contract had a rider that every dressing room must have a Superstation feed.

Elton is an excessive kind of guy, with past alcohol and drug issues, but in the Atlanta Braves he found a non-destructive way to channel some of his enormous energy and emotion. He fell in love with the ballteam, and the game.

During concerts, he told me, he wears an earpiece to listen to the Braves play-by-play. If it's a playoff game, he delays the concert until the game is over.

He gave me an in-depth analysis of his ballclub. It was Millwood this and Furcal that, and "They should move Chipper to third base."

Which they eventually did.

Elton was throwing out stats, discussing the rotation, explaining why the Braves play better at night, why Leyritz kills 'em.

It was surreal, and it flashed through my mind that this might be an elaborate hoax. I actually looked to see if Elton had a little crib sheet. It was the most incongruous baseball interview I'd done since interviewing Richard Nixon back in the '70s. Nixon was very knowledgeable, too, but he seemed to be showing off a little, trying hard to be a baseball dude, with the facts and stats he memorized.

With Elton it was a pure childlike enthusiasm and a deep concern for his boys. He went on and on, excited to have found someone willing to listen to his opinions and theories about the Braves.

"Furcal is really ready to start right now," Elton said, clearly exasperated. "They're trying to baby him too much. Why they are, it's beyond me."

It was Elton John channeling Peter Gammons.

John told me he goes to Braves' games whenever he can and be visits with the players in the clubhouse, chats with Bobby Cox, then slips into a luxury box and keeps a detailed box score. He likes Cox but isn't reluctant to second-guess him.

"You know," Elton said, "just the other day I was talking to Bobby's Cox... Uh-oh, I guess everyone's going to think that's a Freudian slip."

It was a delightful interview and he thanked me, as if he were excited and relieved to have come out of the closet as a Braves fan.

I ran into him again a few months later at another charity event. He rushed up to me, didn't say hello, just grabbed my arm and said, "Didn't I *tell* you about Furcal?"

Rick Pitino

You learn more about life in the second half.

chapter 22

LIVE, DEATH AND HOOPS

Many coaches seem oblivious to life outside of their little bubble, but usually that's an illusion, or a self-delusion. Greatness doesn't exempt you from life, as Rick Pitino learned.

Pitino was coaching at Providence in '87 when his son Daniel died during childbirth. Rick was on the road with the team and the driver pulled the bus to the side of the road so an assistant coach could break the news to Pitino.

For him, coaching became a meaningless exercise. But a man's got to work, and life goes on, so Pitino kept coaching, and gradually he got his chops back. From Providence he went to Kentucky, where he won a national championship in '96, then he jumped to the NBA.

Pitino coached the New York Knicks, then the Boston Celtics for two seasons. The latter experience was the one major failure on his coaching resume, a complete bust, and he started feeling sorry for himself, feeling lost.

"I've lost my bearings and my career," he said on the show a few years later, recalling that time. "I've lost my reputation. What is defeat? What is real loss?"

Pitino left Boston, went back to college ball, at Louisville, whereupon a series of events shook his life.

Rick was in New York with his brother-in-law, who was visiting from out of town. The brother-in-law was trying to hail a cab but a motorist didn't see him standing in the street and hit him, killing him instantly.

Rick's best friend since high school was a guy named Billy Minardi. They were basketball teammates and buddies, and when Rick married Billy's sister, the joke was that Rick married Joan just to stay close to Billy.

When Rick became a big-time coach, he and Billy stayed close. Billy helped Rick with scouting and recruiting in the New York area, and they talked frequently. When Rick would become despondent or discouraged, he would phone Billy.

Billy was a day trader, he worked for Cantor Fitzgerald at the World Trade Center, and you can probably guess where this story goes. Billy was in the North Tower on the morning of September 11 and he never got out.

About the same time, Rick's best player died of cancer, and on the golf course one day Rick doubled over in pain. His doctored suspected prostrate cancer (it turned out to be a nerve problem).

Rick did much soul-searching and made a decision. He would continue coaching, but he would never let anything matter to him more than his family and his friends. He knew if he talked about this that some people would by cynical, would roll their eyes, but he was sincere.

As we talked on the show, Pitino became emotional, his eyes welled up. He talked about how he looked at life as a double-edged sword – so meaningless, and yet you have to struggle to make it meaningful.

"I live too fast," he told me. "We all learn these lessons so late in life. Slow down. Enjoy your life and try to really enjoy what it has to offer."

Rick couldn't bear that his pal Billy might have died in vain, that his name would fade from memory. So Rick established an educational center at the University of Louisville, the Minardi Center, with health care facilities for the elderly and programs for at-risk kids.

From tragedy, Rick sought meaning.

"My son Daniel will be remembered by my doing good things and trying to make life more than just basketball," Rick said.

Rick had just turned 50 when we did that show and he said, "I'm just learning that nothing is owed to you, that success isn't owed to you."

He learned that happiness and success and meaning is something you have to work to achieve and to find, and if there's one thing Rick Pitino could always do, it was work.

With George Steinbrenner

Mark Cuban

Mouths that roar...and sometimes make sense.

chapter

23

KING GEORGE & ANOTHER ROYAL PAIN

You've heard the expression, "Money talks?"

Exhibits A and B: George Steinbrenner and Mark Cuban.

Steinbrenner is the poster boy for crazy money in sports-the monster salaries, heartbreaking ticket prices, runaway appreciation of franchise values.

And when it comes to shoveling your personal fortune into sport and then inserting your voice into the discussion, Dallas Mavericks owner Mark Cuban gives Steinbrenner a run for his money.

Both these fellows skipped charm school and went straight to the power-wielding class. Both are fascinating, hard-driving and obsessed.

Steinbrenner bought the Yankees in '74 for $10 million. In '99 he was offered $550 million to sell. The Yankees are now worth over $1 billion. Baseball's been very-very good to George. As for whether he's been good for baseball, that's a matter of debate.

When I finally got George to sit down with me, I asked him why he'd been so elusive.

"That's by design, Roy. I don't want anyone talking to me."

And he doesn't, in the sense that he picks his spots. If he's got a message to get out, he's available. For a man who said he was going to stay in the background as an owner, he's spent a ton of time in the foreground.

I said, "I appreciate you doing this, but I gotta start with your quote from 1974..."

"Oh, boy, here it comes."

"This is from your press conference when you bought the Yankees. You said, 'I plan absentee ownership. I will not spread myself too thin, I will not be involved in the day-to-day operations of the team. I have enough headaches with the shipping industry.'"

Steinbrenner laughed, then said, "You don't understand, Roy. I walked into that room in New York, and in Cleveland (where he owned a pro basketball team in the old ABL) you might have had two people. Here were 100 people, some of them great writers you've admired your whole life, and I wasn't a welcome character, either. I was from Cleveland, I wasn't a New Yorker.

"Let's remember what Cleveland was at the time. The head of the school board had just been arrested for mooning on the turnpike. The Cuyahoga River had just caught fire. And here's this guy Cleveland, Steinbrenner, who's gonna own the great New York Yankees. The critics were brutal at first, they criticized me everywhere I went. I have to say they've been great to me lately. I have a theory – you work your way up through failure.

"I learned something a long time ago and I have it on my desk: Lead, follow, or get the hell out of the way. In all those years, the thing I'm proudest of is that the Yankees have won more games than any other team in baseball. You know, I used to run track, and I wasn't very good, I was one of the slowest men on my team. But I always hated the red and white ribbons. I was only into the blue ribbon. Since I was a kid, I never wanted anything less than the blue ribbon."

I tossed George some adjectives that have been applied to him.

Intolerant.

"Absolutely."

Generous.

"Aw, I don't know about that."

Harsh.

"Harsh is good."

Control freak

"I hate to use the word freak, but control is a quality I admire. I have to have control."

Tough.

"Tough is good."

Sentimental.

"Aw, I don't want to talk about it."

"A lot of team owners," I said, "have been successful who have stayed out of the public eye, like Walter O'Malley."

"We're different people," George said. "You want to know something amazing? We went to the same school together. Culver Military Academy, along with Lou Nipper, the Reds' owner."

Why are you in the public eye and they weren't?

"I don't know, maybe I wanted the public eye more because I thought it would help me succeed."

Twenty-two managers in 24 years.

"That's right. But I had Billy Martin five times. I had 16 general managers, but the important thing is I stayed with 'em, every one of those guys was taken care of after they got out.

"On the day he died, Billy Martin was on my payroll. The only guy I ever took off my payroll was Dick Hawser, because he went to the Royals. When he died, it was a tough thing, but I paid off his mortgage. I don't want people to say I was a great guy, there's many days I've said I was wrong, and I've carried a lot of bad decisions around, but the bottom line is I feel like I stand up for my players and the people in my organization, even though I'm murderously tough on them."

Did you feel guilty or defeated when Billy Martin was killed, because you couldn't help him with the alcoholism?

"I worked so hard with Billy. I did everything I could. I tried to get him in rehab, tried to get him sober. I threatened to fire him, hired him again. But I couldn't be around all the time, and the truth is (and here Steinbrenner got emotional) I do feel I failed him and his family because I couldn't get him turned around. But ultimately, Billy had to do it for himself, and he couldn't do it."

Your relationship with Reggie Jackson. Up or down?

"My door is always open to Reggie, because Reggie delivered. We have our ups and downs, but Reggie will always have a place in the organization."

What about Dave Winfield? Do you regret the Howard Spira blackmail business?

"Tremendously. It was the biggest mistake of my life. I have great respect for Dave Winfield, and that was me at my worst. And I have to tell you something. I hate to be vilified, because I like to think of myself as a good guy. I'm a tough guy, but I'm a good guy. But you gotta accept that you're always going to be vilified. I take comfort that when I walk down the street in New York, cabdrivers, bartenders, doormen, they all say, 'George, thank you, you're doing a hell of a job.' And I feel vindicated by that."

What does power mean to you?

"I like power, but I like power to do good for other people."

What about courage and loyalty?

"The greatest quality in life is courage. The military, they're the ones with the courage. Everyone else can get in the back of the line."

What do you fear?

"I fear defeat, but I love the battle. I think, ultimately, I've been a good leader. I'd like to have been more like Patton, people called me Patton in pinstripes. But when all is said and done and people ask you, 'Did you serve in the military?,' I can say, 'I served in the Pacific,' but the guys who served under Patton always say, 'I served under Patton.

"My guys, I like the idea that not necessarily did they serve under Steinbrenner, but they wore the pinstripes. It's a sense of immortality, they'll always say, 'I was a Yankee.'"

Final question. If you could say one thing you'd like people to remember about you.

"I'd just like 'em to say, 'He never stopped trying.'"

* * *

Mark Cuban is 30 years younger than Steinbrenner, and richer, and an even bigger pain in the tush to the commissioner of his sport. He's a man in such a hurry to change the world that he was starting businesses at age 12, and he dropped out of high school to go to college. Since buying the Mavericks in 2000, he has been fined more than $1 million for criticizing referees and league procedure.

Cuban sees himself as something of a caped crusader for improvement of his team and of the league. He has the time, money and enthusiasm to stand behind his cause. Cuban is worth about $2.5 billion (with a B). Until he married he lived in a 25,000 square-foot mansion with no furniture, no butler or cook, and only TV dinners in the freezer. He bought a $40 million jet off the internet.

Mavericks' players love Cuban because he bought them the finest plane, equips their lockers with electronic toys and bath towels fit for royalty. Fans love him because he sits in every seat in the house, and personally responds to about 1,000 of their emails every day.

For one of our interviews, I was at Cuban's home as he downloaded his mail.

"You read every one?" I asked.

"Every one of them, yeah. These are customers of the Mavericks and of the NBA, or potential customers, and I would be doing the business a disservice if I didn't see what was on their mind."

And here's a critic. Read that one for us.

"'I agree with you that there are inequities in the NBA when it comes to officiating. And it goes beyond simple human error, or bad officiating. While I appreciate and even admire the passion you have for your team, I believe your actions take away from the issues you raise. Your behavior allows the media to portray you as a crybaby, a crazed crybaby, which in turn allows league officials to easily dismiss you. Why haven't you taken a more rational, reasonable approach when addressing the problem with the league?'"

Okay.

"And my response to her is going to be, 'I've tried many, many times to do this privately behind the scenes. There's not an issue that I have raised publicly that I haven't raised privately dozens of times. And apparently, so far the only response from the NBA comes when something is published."

Now Jerry Buss doesn't answer email like this. Jerry Colangelo doesn't, Abe Pollan doesn't.

"Hopefully they have people who do it for them... You don't know what needs you have unless you've participated in the process and in the business. I have to understand the business, how the customers feel... It's an education. It's communication."

How does money change your life? Do you feel more pressure?

"No. When you've been in the position when the bill collectors are calling you every day, and there's been many a time when I couldn't get a credit card. It's funny, even after I had a billion dollars, I got turned down for one credit card because they went all the way back to look at some of the old bad credit. That was interesting."

You had a friend, or somebody you knew...

"Somebody I was getting to be friends with, yeah."

He asked you for a quarter of a million dollars. You laid it out and never saw him again?

"Well, I didn't write the check. I thought about it for a millisecond. In the course of a conversation he said, 'You know, I don't want to bother you with this, it's no big deal, but I had this bad business deal. Can you write me a check for $250,000?' Before his voice echoed off the wall, I just turned around and walked away, and I haven't seen him since."

I heard some unbelievable things about you. That you sold garbage bags door-to-door.

"When I was 12 years old, to get gym shoes, yeah."

Do you remember the hungry years vividly?

"Oh, yeah! When I first came to Dallas I lived with six guys in a three-bedroom apartment. I didn't have my own bed, I had a crusty pillow and a blanket I would put my stuff under. When we didn't have any money, we would kite checks to each other. So I'd write him a check, and he'd write him a check, and he'd write him one, and then the last guy would write the rent check, knowing it would take time for all this to hit.

"I remember eating mustard and ketchup sandwiches."

Were you a disco-dance teacher?

"In college, yeah. Hey, let's put it this way: If someone offered you $25 an hour to go into a sorority and teach them all how to dance, would you say no?"

We talked about the way he treats his players. Each player's locker has a DVD, a flat-screen TV, a leather recliner.

And the towels, I've never seen towels like this. Are you running a country club here?

"Well, let's put it this way: Guys have no excuses And if they don't produce, they're gone. I've said it very specifically to the guys. I'm not loyal to players, I'm loyal to the ring. Anybody who works for me, whether you're a receptionist or a player, I'm going to do everything possible to put you in a position to succeed. But we all have to keep our eyes on the prize."

One might argue that you're coddling them.

"I hope so. Do you know anyone who doesn't want to be coddled at work?"

But they're paid millions of dollars, these guys... Here's a question: Why do you think owners spend millions and millions of dollars for ballplayers, and then nickel-and-dime them in the back end?

"I have no idea. But I hope they do. And I hope they continue doing it. It's just a better opportunity for me. When I first got the team I had a meeting with the players and I said, okay guys, gripe session. What's on your mind. Gary Trent stands up and says, 'Mark, after games on the road we wind up at three in the morning, like in Oakland, at hotels with no room service. Do you want us roaming the streets of Oakland looking for a Subway?'"

So what would you do? Hire a caterer?

"No, we started staying in hotels that cost me nine dollars more a night per room, hotels that offered 24-hour room service. You know, just basic Good Business 101... If I have a $50 million payroll, and spend half a million in perks, which is basically what happens, to optimize the value of that payroll, I'm a moron if I don't do it."

Cuban formed a great partnership with another NBA eccentric, coach Don Nelson, now an advisor. Weird things happened. They gave Dennis Rodman a shot when every other team recoiled. That didn't work. But many of Nelson's unconventional ideas helped make the Mavs a genuine contender and a crowd favorite around the league.

"He's very creative, he's always open to change. When I first met him, the first question I asked him was, 'Don, are you having fun?' And he said 'No.' And I said, 'Well, that's my first job, to make this fun. Let's put everyone around you in a position to succeed and put you in a position to succeed. All I ask is that you be brutally honest with me, and no matter how dumb a question I ask, you give me an answer, so I can learn.

"He's willing to try anything to win. The Hack-a-Shaq, perfect example."

But if *your* player was getting hacked, you'd be saying that they're not calling it enough, that they're endangering his health.

"Hell, no. You know what I'd say? I say to our player, 'We have a free-throw coach, get your ass here early and learn how to shoot free throws.'"

Cuban's on-going battle with NBA commissioner David Stern is seen by some as a manifestation of Cuban's immaturity or even insanity.

If you knew what you were saying or doing could in any way hurt this game, would you finally shut up?

"Yeah, yeah, yeah!"

But you've never felt that?

"No, not ever. It's the exact opposite. Everything, every bit of training I've ever had just puts up a big red flag saying, 'Boy, there's things here we better be careful about."

Why bang your head against the wall? It's getting you nowhere.

"When I look at how the NBA as a business is being run, whether it's the officiating group or other groups, I see all kinds of red flags...I'd rather do what I believe and think is right and go down in flames. Everybody says this is the way it's been done for fifty years. My goodness, you know, how could you challenge that? Or, 'There's 28 other guys (owners) who aren't doing this, why are you?' Usually that's an indication I'm doing something right."

Cuban feels that Stern is a genius when it comes to such matters as negotiating TV contracts and union-labor agreements. But Cuban's main complaint about Stern is that he runs the league without input from the owners as a group.

"The NBA doesn't communicate information at all. It's like a private society in all respects. I don't even know how much David Stern gets paid."

Are you chasing windmills, a little bit?

"I don't think so. I mean, it's not like I haven't challenged businesses before. It's not like I haven't been involved in businesses where people have been powerful. I've competed against IBM. I've competed against Microsoft. I've had a guy sit in front of me and say, 'Mark, I raised a hundred million dollars, just to put you out of business.' He was gone within six months. So that (intimidation) is not enough incentive for me to back down."

NBA owners are all successful people. Jerry Buss, Paul Allen, Jim Dolan. Yet they don't shout, they don't scream, they don't get fined.

"And they don't go to league meetings anymore, either."

And you find that "very tell-tale." Why do you think they don't go?

"I know why. Because what's the point? The agenda is already set when you get there. Now I'm really going to get in trouble (he laughs)."

Cuban feels that all the fines and reprimands from the league should be seen by the public as a sign that something is amiss, other than inside his own head.

"You know, the more the emperor shouts and screams and yells, and fines, the more it raises questions. I've said to David many times, dozens of times, I'm the easiest guy in the NBA to shut up. The easiest! Just take some simple actions. You know, if I question the officiating, the way the officials are managed, bring in a third party. I promise I will sign on a dotted line that I won't ever use the word referee or official ever in a sentence again."

You don't want to be king. You just want a better kingdom.

"Yes, that's it!"

With Cal Ripken, Jr.

An iron man with a pen.

24

SIGNING YOUR LIFE AWAY

The autograph was once simple and pure, a Norman Rockwell moment, a one-on-one interaction between a player and a kid.

Babe Ruth signed a million autographs, and usually added a bonus wink.

Now the autograph process has all the warmth of an ATM withdrawal.

Where did we go wrong?

Here's my two cents worth:

If you're an athlete, you should sign autographs for at least 20 minutes before or after your event or appearance. And not just when the cameras are rolling. Stop your car and sign a few on your way out of the parking lot, instead of hiding behind your smoked windows.

It's one way of thanking the fans for their support, their admiration, and the fact that they pay your salary. Don't blow off those kids by mumbling "I have to do my work." That *is* your work.

Autograph shows suck the last ounce of soul out of the player-fan interaction. I've been to autograph shows and seen signs like, "Do not engage in conversation with Mr. Mays. He will sign flats only. Do not ask him to personalize unless you want to pay another $39.95."

These athletes should be on their hands and knees giving thanks that someone wants their signature.

And fellas, try to find it in your heart to glance up once in a while and make eye contact with that kid holding the scorecard, his jaw dropped in amazement that he's this close to his hero. The autograph will be lost in a week, but your glance will last him a lifetime. Remember the Babe's wink.

And you, Joe Fan, try not to act like a crazed stalker. Say please, don't crush the little kid in front of you, and try not to hold a lifetime grudge if the player has to cut off his signing session before he gets to you.

The whole process has become so dehumanizing and dreary. I wish every athlete could take a class on class from Cal Ripken Jr.

I took my son to an Orioles game at Anaheim during Ripken's final season. During batting practice, Andy and I were sitting in the Baltimore dugout when I heard someone call my name. It was Ripken, he was standing at the railing of the grandstands, signing autographs.

"Hey, Roy," he said, "toss me a few balls."

I didn't know why he wanted the balls, but Andy and I picked up a few and tossed 'em to Cal. Then I noticed a huge commotion in the grandstands near where Ripken was signing. A team of paramedics was working on someone, there were police all around, and a little ambulance cart arrived.

Cal kept on signing, autograph after autograph, dozens of 'em. And he's a slow autographer. Most guys just scribble, but Cal writes his name carefully then blows on it to dry the ink.

Well, it turned out that a woman who had been waiting for Cal's autograph suffered a heart attack right there, basically stopped breathing. The paramedics arrived quickly, used the de-fib paddles to bring her back, then loaded her onto the ambulance cart.

Cal took the baseballs Andy and I tossed him, signed them, and gave them to the paramedics – one for each of them and one for the woman (she survived, by the way). Then he just kept on signing for all the kids, as if people had heart attacks all the time while waiting for Cal's autograph.

Later I asked him, "How do you do that, just keep signing after something horrible like that happens?"

Cal said, "I can't just go back to the dugout and put my head in my hands, Roy. Those people are waiting for an autograph."

The spirit of the Bambino lives.

With Brett Favre

Going way beyond X's and O's.

chapter
25

BEHIND THE GLAMOR
OF THE QUARTERBACK

Warren Sapp was on the show, and Warren has a sweetheart side but he can scare people. I asked him if he would want his sister to marry an NFL player.

"No!" Sapp yelled, laughing.

Then he was quiet for a moment, he was thinking.

"Trent Dilfer," he said, very firmly.

Dilfer is a quarterback, a pretty boy, a religious man, while Sapp is a lineman, a man of the trenches, a man who makes a living hating and hurting quarterbacks. These two men are so opposite in so many ways, yet Sapp was saying he would want his sister to marry Dilfer.

"Why Dilfer?" I asked. Trent Dilfer hadn't even been part of our discussion.

"'Cause Dilfer, it wouldn't bother Dilfer if he was in love with a black woman. Dilfer could transfer from (relate to) me to you, opposite personalities. Dilfer was the best teammate ever! Ever in life, Dilfer's the best! 'Cause Dilfer would do everything… Dilfer would play cards with us (linemen), gamble with us, everything, didn't bother (if we were) black, white, Mexican, he was everybody's guy. Dilfer's the best!"

Never mind that Dilfer is already happily married, Sapp gave him a hell of an endorsement, and it came out of the blue, but I'm going to tell you why I wasn't surprised.

Because Dilfer is a hero. A hero is someone with the gift or the ability, and the character and courage, to uplift another human being, especially under adverse circumstances.

Trent Dilfer – and Brett Favre – are heroes, although both of them would decline the tile. They prefer to bestow the hero honors on people who have lifted them. Favre credits the development of his character to his father, mother and his wife, and Dilfer owes his debt to his son, who died at age five, and to a "rival" quarterback.

Dilfer and Favre both express unqualified love for their teammates. Next time someone tries to tell you football isn't a team game, that locker room relationships don't matter, refer them to this chapter.

Sometimes great quarterbacks become great quarterbacks because they have strong arms and quick brains. But I'm convinced that there's much more that goes into the make-up of a man who leads a team to greatness. I offer as evidence these two gentlemen and their response to personal tragedy.

Trent Dilfer is no Hall of Famer but he wears a Super Bowl ring earned by leading the 2000 Baltimore Ravens to the NFL title, and his fellow players voted him to a Pro Bowl that season.

Some background: Dilfer played at Fresno State, where he was everybody's All-American Party Dude. Let's just say Trent extended Happy Hour. He ran up huge bar tabs around Fresno and never paid 'em, because he was the quarterback.

One day he decided, in a half-ass way, to join an on-campus Bible study group. Trent was usually the only person at the meeting with a killer hangover, but he kept going and one day a bell rang in his head and he decided to dedicate his life to his religious faith.

The Tampa Bay Buccaneers drafted Trent in the first round, the sixth overall pick. He became the first Buccaneer quarterback to be voted to the Pro Bowl, but the Bucs released him.

Trent signed with the Baltimore Ravens, a team built around the defensive greatness of Ray Lewis. After the Ravens won the

Super Bowl title, they released Dilfer, solidifying his rep as being competent enough not to mess up a great defensive team. Not a great player, but an adequate caretaker of the QB position.

That's his public rep, but his teammates tell you different. Sapp's endorsement is typical. The players truly respect this guy. To Trent, the son of a football coach, football isn't X's and 0's, it's brotherhood.

Trent told me, "They're gonna have to drag me out of the NFL by my toenails, because it's too special, the relationships you make in this league and the adversity you go through and the struggle… I love the game, but I love the team aspect, the camaraderie, the relationships."

However, as Trent told me in our interview, there was a time he was going to quit, walk away. It was at his next NFL stop, Seattle. Dilfer was signed as a fill-in for injured starter Matt Hasselbeck, but Trent revved up the team, and was pronounced the starting quarterback by coach Mike Holmgren. Almost immediately Dilfer ruptured an Achilles tendon and blew out a knee.

Trent decided to retire. He was set financially, he'd been knocked around and beat up. Why not call it a career while he could still walk, spend quality time with his wife Cassandra and their four children – three girls and a boy?

Their son, Trevin, was five at the time. He'd been in dad's arms in the locker room after the Super Bowl, baptized by championship champagne. Trevin was blessed with an abundance of energy and joy. He was dynamic and competitive, he became a favorite of Trent's teammates.

The family took a trip to Disneyland and the kids loved it, but Trevin fell ill, began running a high fever. They took him to a doctor, who said it was probably a virus, then maybe a strain of hepatitis.

Then Trevin collapsed. Doctors wanted to medivac him to Stanford Medical Center but this was the first month of the Iraqi war so there were no helicopters available. On the long ambulance ride to Palo Alto, Trevin's heart stopped twice, and at the hospital he was placed on life support, kept alive on lung and heart machines.

Trevin had a severe viral infection of the heart. He would need a heart transplant in order to survive.

Dilfer got on his knees and begged God to let him trade his life for his son's, straight-up. But Trevin kept losing weight and slipped into a coma. Every day 40 to 50 people, many of them Trent's teammates, visited Trevin. Finally the doctors told the Dilfers that it was too late for a transplant, that Trevin would never recover, would always be in a coma. They had to decide.

Trent prayed, and he felt God telling him he had to let go, so Trent and Cassandra ordered doctors to pull the plug.

In our interview I asked Trent about that time of grieving, and why he decided to come back to football.

"After I lost my son," he said, "after a month or so I started wondering if I was gonna keep playing, and inside I wanted to, but as anyone who has faced any type of depression in their life knows, just because you want to do something doesn't mean that you can get up and do it every day.

"It wasn't working out. I just came off the Achilles tear so I had no function in my right leg, and the thought of leaving my family for an extended period of time, I just couldn't imagine it. I decided about three days before training camp that I was going to retire.

"Sitting on the couch one night, my wife was saying, 'Are you sure? We're behind you if you want to play.' So she got me thinking. Well, that night Matt (Hasselbeck) calls me, like he heard our conversation on the couch. We had talked a bunch after I lost my son, so it wasn't unusual that he called, and he just started telling me how much the team needs me. And he's so excited for training camp because of the impact I have on the football team, and how they need to see me, and how they're grieving to a certain degree, and to see me at training camp would lift the spirits of the team, and they were going to be there for me.

"Then he said something that I'll try to say without crying. He said, 'You know, Trent' – and this was a huge year for him, this was the year he had to produce or he wasn't going to be the quarterback for Seattle – and he said, 'You know, I thought a lot about my goals for the season, and my number one goal is to be the best friend you've ever had. I don't care what happens in training camp. I don't care if I have a good camp or a bad camp, if I get hurt or I'm healthy, I will be there for you this training camp.'

"That he *thought* about that was amazing, and then he *did* it. There were nights in training camp, and I haven't told many people this, but I just wouldn't sleep. Matt and I would stay up goofing around and what not. There'd be times he had to get some sleep so I'd leave and go into my room, and I just couldn't sleep, I'd be up crying or something. And he would knock on my door at 4 in the morning. 'You're not sleeping, are you?' 'No.' 'Let's play a video game.'

"I mean, we averaged two, maybe three, hours of sleep a night that entire training camp, and here he is going into the biggest year of his career and he could care less how he felt the next morning for football. He wanted to make sure I had a distraction, or could laugh, or talk, or just lose my mind in a video game.

"And I would take a bullet for him for that, because he saved my career... him and my wife."

I asked Trent to talk about Trevin.

"He called himself Trevin to the Rescue. He loved his superheroes, like every five-year-old, but he didn't want to be Spiderman or Superman, he wanted to be his own superhero, and he named himself Trevin to the Rescue, and he really believed that he could rescue his sisters from any problems. He always cared more about people around him than himself. He was gonna be an offensive lineman, because he had that mentality, he was into protecting people.

"So when he got sick and he was on life support, and we took him off his medication to make sure his brain function was all right, he could tear up, he could blink and he could squeeze your finger. And what he reacted to was when his sisters were in the room, and they were crying, that hurt him. When I got like this (crying), you could see him tear up because he was sad for me. He just had so much courage, such a big heart."

I mentioned to Trent that he is a deeply religious man and he believes Trevin is in good hands.

He said, "I thought, 'What is a way I can honor him?' And really, the one thing that I've tried to do, and nobody would know, but when we come in from warming up, there's usually about a 10-minute period where it's somewhat quiet, guys are fixing their pads, making sure everything's right. And I go and find a corner and I just pray. 'Lord, I know Trevin's sitting right there with you. Give him a front-row seat today.' I just pray that through my attitude, my actions and my words today, that he would be proud of me."

* * *

Brett Favre's story has parallels with Dilfer's. They were both sons of high school football coaches, both were knucklehead party guys who eventually found sobriety and forms of spirituality, both fought through much personal pain, and both believe in the ultimate glory of the team.

Dilfer battled alcohol, Favre battled booze and an addiction to pain-relief drugs. In '96 Favre spent 45 days in a rehab clinic and has been stone-sober since.

Favre has dealt with tragedy. His father, who was also his high school coach, died in 2003. His brother-in-law was killed in a vehicle accident on Brett's ranch in Louisiana, and Brett's wife began battling breast cancer in 2003, before finally receiving a clean bill of health two years later.

Where Dilfer had Hasselbeck, Favre had Reggie White, the late, great defensive end. Before they were teammates, White gave Favre the hardest hit he ever took, a sack that separated Brett's shoulder. But when White joined the Packers, a bond was formed.

"There was not a better teammate," Brett told me. "I've learned a lot from Reggie, and part of my speech when my father passed away probably came from him, subconsciously. Talking about your dedication to your teammates, to your team, because Reggie left it all on the field.

"Reggie was a great family man, and when I was a knucklehead (battling addiction), he was right there beside me. When he was walking a straight line, I was zigzagging and he was always there to pick me up. And I guess it's kind of like the mother's love for her son. Regardless of what the son does, she loves him, and that's the way Reggie was, not only with me but with other players.

"He could have been like I've been in the past, when you turn your back on someone and you go, 'If you don't want to do it this way, then so be it.' He wasn't like that."

Brett told me he doesn't like to look back with regret, but he does look back with amazement at the years and memories he lost to alcohol and pills.

"I can't believe I won three MVPs and I hardly remember those seasons," he said. "I was taking 15 Vicodins, I was drinking, I was neglecting not only myself but I was hurting people around me. Yet I was playing at the top of my game.

"When I quit drinking and taking the pain medication, I remember going to stadiums and fans would be yelling, 'Hey, Favre, you need more pills,' or, 'You need another beer.' And our security staff and players would want to go up there and fight these people, and I would think, 'There is nothing out there that would make me want to do that (drink or take pills) again. I don't care how many touchdown passes I could possibly throw or how many more Super Bowls I could go through, I feel so much better in my life.'"

Favre led the Packers to a Super Bowl title, but the greatest game he ever played – maybe the greatest game any quarterback ever played – was a relatively meaningless regular-season game in Oakland in the winter of '03, the day after his father died.

Irving Favre and his son Brett were connected at the heart by football. "We talked football all the way home from (high school) practice," Brett said a few years ago. "We talked football at suppertime, we talked football before bed. We talked football when we got up in the morning."

And they talked football throughout Brett's NFL career. Irving was part of the Packer family. He was in the locker room before almost every game, traveled to most away games, and he was friends with everyone from the owner to the water boy. You could often find Irving in Green Bay's humblest working-class saloons, sharing beers and football talk with Cheeseheads. Irving and Brett still talked ball constantly.

Irving died at age 58 of a heart attack on a Sunday, and Brett played the next night against the Raiders. Here is an excerpt from a column written by Scott Ostler of the *San Francisco Chronicle*.

> *Brett played Monday night against the Raiders, the first time since fifth grade that his father wasn't at his game. He played not so much for his own grief therapy, but because the Packers count on him and they're fighting for a playoff spot.*
>
> *If there was a lesson Irving Favre pounded home to his son over the years, by his actions and his words, it was this: Don't get cheated out of your swings. Live life. The meek might inherit the earth, but they won't stand up to a good pass rush and they won't be much fun at the post-game party. Don't waste a play, don't waste a day. And whatever you do, don't let your team down.*
>
> *Brett had help carrying his burden Monday night. It's doubtful there is a player in the NFL or any sport who has the absolute love, admiration and respect of his teammates that Favre has.*

It's a game that spoke to the character of the man, and his family. Brett's mother was a special-education teacher and Brett told me, "It always seemed like I related better to mentally-challenged kids."

Irving Favre coached American Legion baseball and the batboy was a mentally-challenged man named Ronnie who was Irving's age and who lived with the Favres. Brett and Ronnie shared a bedroom for several years. Ronnie rode a bicycle around town and Brett thought of him as just another pal.

"Except at 4:30 in the morning when he wanted to go get coffee," Brett said. "A 15-year-old kid doesn't want coffee at 4:30 in the morning."

In our interview I asked Brett about that game against the Raiders. He said the decision to play was easy, but playing was hard. It was the only time in his NFL career, including his first game and his Super Bowl game, that he was nervous sick.

"The problem was that playing was only half the battle," Brett said. "Just playing, to me, was not good enough... Mike (coach Holmgren) is sittin' in the hotel room with me and I'm cryin'. I'm laughin'. I'm cryin'. Players are comin' in and out. Mike was by my side the whole time. He said, 'You want to go home? We would love to have you, we need you, but no one's ever going to blink an eye if you go home.'

"I thought about it for 30 seconds and said no. I gotta play. I gotta play. And I'm not big on speaking, but that night I spoke to our team and it was one of the toughest things I ever had to do, but it was probably the best talk I have ever given in my life. It just came out... I looked out to these guys and was fighting to hold back tears, because I wanted to get through it. I mean, it was just quiet. There were guys who were cryin'.

"I was tryin' not to upset anyone, but I can remember saying, 'Guys, if you ever questioned my commitment to this team or to this game, you'll never question it again. My dad meant a lot to me off the field, but he meant just as much on the field. That's the reason I'm here today and I'm going to play tomorrow, and I don't want you to play for me or play for my dad. I want you to play for this team because that's what I'm going to do. And I've always told you guys I do whatever it would take to win, and here's a perfect example, and I don't want you to feel sorry for me.'

"I was afraid to fail. People said, 'Well, he (your dad) was there watching, he was on your shoulder.' Something happened in that game, because I was so scared and I never played with that type of emotion. Not too many good things can happen when you're scared to play bad, and so I thought, 'Maybe I'm making a mistake,' but I knew I couldn't back away at that point. I couldn't go in and take my uniform off."

Favre threw four touchdown passes and completed 22 of 30 passes. *In the first half!* The Packers won.

It's a matter of character.

"You know," Brett told me, "success can do one of two things, in my opinion. It can change you for the better or it can change you for the worse. My wife and family have changed me for the better…

"People say, 'What do you want people to remember you as?' It's simple for me, and I think it kinda sums up my career and my personality and the way I treat other people. I want people not to say, 'He was a great quarterback.' I want people to say, 'He played the game one way, he played the damn game the way I would have wanted to play it. He seems like he's just a regular guy who has a uniform on.'

"Because that's me. It may be that early in my career or early in my life I wasn't that guy. But I evolved into that guy because of the people around me. Because I was able to see that sometimes guys have blinders on and you are only able to see one thing – me, me, me.

"And there came a time in my life where I wanted to treat people better. I wanted to treat everyone as equals. I wanted to treat my teammates as friends and show them that I cared about them, as opposed to 'What's my stats, What did I do?' None of that stuff matters anymore, and it won't matter 20 years from now. What matters is what type of guy you are, and if you are ever in need, you want people to come knockin' on your door. And hopefully I've done that."

Larry Greene

My friend. A true original.

LEAPIN' LARRY

You've never heard of Larry Greene. He was a friend of mine, a news photographer. He worked for CBS news and was killed several years ago in a helicopter crash while filming a news story in Syria. Larry always made a lot of noise, but he was a quiet hero. I gave the following eulogy at his funeral.

* * *

I was trying to read the five o'clock news on the radio station. I was trying to give it my best radio-newsman voice. You know, the deep nasal voice that a college kid thinks will get him a professional job, but it never does.

Here I was in the newsroom of the college station, thinking I was important, talking about Watergate, trying to sound like I knew what I was doing, reading from my script. I thought I was the coolest sophomore at the University of Miami. I had a journalism career underway. Just then I looked up and there, pressed against the studio glass, was Larry Greene's bare butt.

Now forgive me, folks, I'm going to tell you about the Larry Greene I knew, because he wouldn't have it any other way.

Leapin' Larry Greene – that was his nickname – was mooning me while I was reading the news on the air. And he was making these hideous faces, grotesque and bizarre. I started laughing so uncontrollably that I lost any pretense of doing the news report. I don't know what it sounded like on the air, but every time I started with, "White House counsel John Dean..." I would blow up with laughter because Leapin' Larry was doing some outrageous, absurd thing against the glass.

I start off with that story because it was the first time l encountered the legendary Larry Greene. Leapin' Larry was a true icon at the University of Miami in the '70s. He was a hippie. He was raunchy. He was dangerous and the most creative radio personality in the school and probably in the country. He was Howard Stern before Howard Stern, and ten times as gutsy. He was like Monty Python and Larry Flynt rolled into one. Sort of Robin Williams in *Good Morning, Vietnam,* only wilder.

This guy would interview prostitutes and strippers and freaks of all kinds, He broadcast his radio show once live from a parachute, while skydiving. That's how he got the name Leapin' Larry.

He was so nervy it was scary. He lived like he broadcast. He was an eccentric. He had pet rats and iguanas that he would put on leashes and walk around campus. No one knew what to do with Larry. And he wasn't just courageous and fearless, he was a threat to the status quo. At first I kind of avoided him, I thought he wasn't safe to be around

And then it happened. A rumor spread that Leapin' Larry's radio show, the Saturday Night Whoopee Show, was going to be cancelled, that he had done something so outrageous that even he had to marvel at the breathtakingly bad taste. He implied on his show that he had used a hidden microphone to record the university president having sex with two prostitutes. Then, as photo editor for the college yearbook, he phonied up a photo that had the same president taking on two hookers.

If this sounds like bad taste, folks, deal with it, because Larry was the Oprah Winfrey of bad taste. He liked bad, stupid, sleazy music and films. That was the Larry I met nearly 30 years ago, the Larry who introduced me to all kinds of contraband – the best blues I would ever listen to, and to one of my heroes, Todd Rundgren, for whom Larry also idolized for his whack ideas.

Larry Greene was more than a Hawkeye Pierce rebel in college He was an almost mythic figure. But he was much more than a dangerous guy. He was a creative whirlwind who hated pretense and couldn't wait to humiliate the pompous.

He was a kind of hero to me, but he really intimidated me, because I thought he was crazy. And he was. But the truth was he wasn't just crazy. He was a jester. The jester is one that makes you laugh and keeps you guessing with pranks and stunts, and then when the smoke clears, you remember not the serious stuff in life but the really fun and daring stuff that makes life so sweet.

The jester and I landed jobs at the CBS affiliate in Miami. And at first I tried to separate myself from him because I knew if he pulled any more of his wild stuff, he would get both of us fired before we had a chance to have a career and I'd never be Dan Rather because of Larry Greene. Guess what? Larry Greene – and he was still Leapin' Larry – won them over at CBS. He became the best photojournalist that they ever had. He taught me how to edit videotape and he loosened me up to such a degree that I no longer feared the daring and outrageous.

There are a few people in this room today who remember Larry in Miami, and all of us have outrageous, wacky Larry stories. He brought porn pictures to camera shoots and would show 'em to the governor and presidential candidates, just to see their eyes bug out. He wanted to get a reaction. They all knew Larry. People like Ted Kennedy, Nelson Rockefeller, Mike Wallace, and guess who else? Dan Rather. They were all fans of Larry, and I think I know why. Because they were tired of their own BS and this guy represented a reprieve from the sad, confining world that most of us live in. These guys always asked for Larry during the political convention in Miami.

We went to California together and got jobs at Channel 2 together and Larry never changed. He was still a great photojournalist and editor. He was still a breath of fresh air.

And I don't want to get too sentimental here, because Larry would have thought it's sappy – he hated it when I got sappy and melodramatic with my reports. But I'm going to tell you something l never got to say to Larry, because I was afraid he'd think it was too sentimental. He was the most passionate, daring and alive guy I ever met in my whole life. There was nobody like him.

I want to tell you a story about the time Larry and I and a guy named Elliot Fons did an interview with Miles Davis for CBS news. I was shocked that Miles Davis immediately took a liking to Leapin' Larry.

We were filming at Davis' house in Malibu and even though Miles had a reputation for being extremely reclusive and very difficult to deal with, he was having a ball with Larry Greene. He stole one of Larry's police badges. Larry collected police badges.

Davis was wearing a red leather fringed jacket, pure Miles, The coat must have cost a fortune. He looks at Larry's badge and says, "Hey, Larry, I like that badge. I want to collect police badges, too." And Larry says, "Miles, you want my badge?" And Miles goes, "Yeah, I'll give you anything for it." Larry says. "Miles, let me get a photo with you, and you can have the badge," Miles says, "No problem. Larry, pin the badge on me." Larry says, "Miles, if I pin this badge on your jacket I'm going to tear the leather." Miles says, "Pin it on, Larry, I don't care." And Larry pins it on, and rips a huge hole in the jacket. Miles doesn't say anything, but Larry is horrified. So am I.

But Miles has this huge smile on his face.

That was 17 years ago, and I'd love to tell you that Larry and I were close friends over the years, but I kind of let life get in the way. God knows, he always put it out to me to get together. He was proud of his boys, Clayton and Connor. He built a skateboard park for them, and always wanted my boys to get together with his. And l really kick myself now, because I would have loved for my boys to meet this special and interesting man named Leapin' Larry. Uncle Leapin' Larry would have had a nice ring to it.

When I heard how he died, I was sad and angry. If those people hadn't attacked the World Trade Center, Leapin' Larry wouldn't have been in the Gulf of Arabia. Larry didn't even like helicopters, he thought they were dangerous. Imagine that, Larry Greene, cautious. He became cautious because he wanted to see his boys grow up to bust his chops, and he wanted to love his wife Diana forever. He used to tell me he couldn't believe how a jerk like him could be married to such a beautiful woman. He wanted to be more careful, not more reckless.

Larry, I'm sorry you are not here. I'm sorry for Diana and the boys. I'm sorry for all of us who knew you, and I'm really sorry for the ones who didn't get to see all the stuff you pulled. I'm sorry the jester won't be with us to make us laugh and astonish us with the strange and inappropriate. Life will be a lot more lonely arid boring without the jester.

Goodbye, Leapin' Larry. I love you.

With Troy Aikman

A true role model's brother.

You are entering the area where the Alfred P. Murrah Building once stood. The granite used on this pathway was salvaged from the Murrah Building. The Field of Empty Chairs is a tribute to the 168 Americans who were killed April 19, 1995. The nine rows represent the nine floors of the former Murrah Building. Each person's chair is positioned in the row that corresponds to the floor on which they worked or were visiting. The five westernmost Empty Chairs honor those who were killed outside the Murrah Building.

chapter
27

TROY'S TRUE HERO

In Oklahoma City, where the Murrah Federal Building stood until it was bombed into rubble on April 19, 1995, there is a beautiful memorial. It includes a long reflecting pool and a grassy field with 168 bronze and stone chairs, each symbolizing a person who died in the attack. Nineteen of the chairs are smaller, representing children.

It is very quiet at the memorial. Oklahoma City is a quiet place anyway, but there is a real stillness at the memorial. One sound you notice is a faint tinkling, the wind rattling the thousands of trinkets and tokens of love and hope that have been placed on a chain-link fence by visitors, and it's an amazing array of objects. A U.S. Hot Rod Monster Jam poster hangs next to a picture of Jesus, next to a boy-sized baseball glove.

It's quiet, but to many who were there when the building was bombed, the noise never goes away. The screams and sirens and sounds of chaos went on for hours, and days, and they echo still.

Tammi Powell was there. Tammi is Troy Aikman's sister, 17 months older than Troy. Cowboys' fans consider Troy Aikman a genuine hero. He took their team to three Super Bowls and won all of them. Hall of Fame. An athlete of dignity, character and courage.

Troy has a hero, too: Tammi. She was one of the rescue and relief workers at the Oklahoma City tragedy, although until I interviewed them both in late '95, Troy wasn't aware of what his sister had done, and the impact it had on her life.

A little background: Growing up, Troy was a great athlete, almost as great as Tammi. They were best friends and they had an on-going athletic rivalry that they thrived on it. They didn't play catch, they played burn-out. They tried to kill one another in ping pong. They lived at the parks and ballfields of Orange County, south of Los Angeles. Tammi played softball and ran track, Troy played everything, and if one had a game, the other was in the stands cheering, along with an older sister, Terri.

When Troy was in eighth grade the family moved to Henryetta, Oklahoma, about 95 miles east of Oklahoma City, and Troy and Tammi became even closer. Everyone knew Troy would become a pro athlete. One day Tammi told her mom that she wanted to become a nurse.

They both attended Oklahoma University. Tammi got her masters, then went to work at a hospital in Oklahoma City. Troy broke his leg in a football game as a freshman, transferred to UCLA, then was drafted by the Cowboys, who have a huge following in Oklahoma.

The morning of the Murrah Building bombing, Tammi's son had chicken pox so she was late for work at St. Anthony's Hospital, six blocks from the Murrah Building. She was heading to work when the bomb went off at 9:01, and somehow she made her way to the hospital, through the smoke and panic and bedlam, arriving at 10:30.

"The thing I'll never forget is the sound," she said. "The sirens were non-stop, all day and night. To this day, whenever I hear a siren of any kind I'm on edge. I can feel it, I can hear it, it never goes away, that sound."

Tammi was assigned to work in the Family Room, and she was there for two days and nights, working non-stop. She was given updated lists of people who had been in the Murrah building and had either escaped or been rescued.

People searching for friends, relatives or loved ones either phoned the Family Room or came in, desperate, panicked. For a few, Tammi had good news. For most, all Tammi could say was, "We don't know. We have no information on that person."

I interviewed Troy and Tammi together in '96 and I asked Tammi what it was like, and she had to pause and take deep breaths. I asked her if she wanted to take a break in the taping, and she shook her head.

"It was very, very hard," she said. "People would come in, there would be total grief, you'd see in their faces the desperation to find a mother or sister or children."

I asked if there were any happy stories. She said she didn't remember any. She said one thing that bothered her was a friend of hers at the hospital, a security guard, who asked Tammi, "Is my mom on the list?" Tammi had to say no, and the guard fell apart, grief-stricken. They never found the guard's mom.

Now it was getting harder for Tammi to talk to me, and she started crying.

She said, "There was a woman who was the aunt of two children, and she kept saying, over and over, 'Where's Chase? Where's Canton? Where's my Chase? Where's my Canton?' They were the same ages as my boys."

Tammi said she carried the names of those boys in her pocket for days, trying to find some clue, trying to find Chase and Canton.

As Tammi took a breath, I asked Troy, "Where were you that day?"

He laughed and said, "You know where I was? Playing in some golf tournament with Steve Beuerlein, a fundraiser. Someone pulled me aside and said, 'Did you hear about the bombing today in Oklahoma City?' Honest to God, Roy, I didn't put two and two together. I'm ashamed to tell you the first thing in my mind wasn't Tammi.

"I knew she was involved, but I figured she was safe because she was at the hospital, but until that interview we did in '95 it just never occurred to me what a hero she was, how traumatic it was, and I'm ashamed to tell you that."

Ten days after the bombing, Cowboys owner Jerry Jones sent Troy and several other Cowboys to Oklahoma City.

"I've never really thought that what we do in football is important," Troy said, "I kind of scoff at people who think what I do is significant in the overall scheme of things. But when I went to visit the site and the hospital, we visited one man who was in very critical condition, hanging by a thread, his body filled with metal shrapnel. He had been drinking a cup of coffee when the bomb went off and it threw him three floors down.

"I go into his room, he's hooked up to every kind of machine, barely conscious, and he looks at me and says, 'Troy Aikman! How the Cowboys gonna do this year?' I was absolutely horrified and embarrassed that I would have any kind of importance in his life, but I also came away feeling and understanding the magnitude of how people look at what we do, and how it gives them something to hang onto when things are horrible.

"That's what I thought of during 9-11, too, when you see all those ballplayers going down to the site, people say, 'It's just a photo op, grandstanding,' But you've got to hear what these people do, and how they react.

"Roy, to tell you the truth, I thought it was just symbolic that we went down there, and I was embarrassed there was a camera crew, and I felt selfish. The truth is, I really feel I got more from them than I could have given, and I felt a confidence in the human spirit, not for me but for how people can endure."

Tammi: "There was an older woman in the hospital, she lost every member of her family, and there was no anger, no bitterness. I can't imagine how I'd react, I like to think I'd react with courage, but I've never seen courage like that before."

Troy: "We talk a lot about courage in sports, then I see what Tammi did and how people had to deal with trauma and tragedy. I think the people who tried to go after the hijackers of that airplane, the people who endured what they did at the World Trade Center and the Pentagon, that is real heroism."

Tammi: "When all is said and done, I really have to believe in my heart that people are good. Some people aren't, but we really need to spend more time focusing on people who are good... I try as much as I can to focus on people who endure, with courage, who overcome. We focus too much on negativity, we don't focus nearly enough on the good, and on our families and lives and commitment to what we do and our friends."

Tammi said she thinks of the bombing every single day and realizes, "There but for the grace of God go I." She wonders, "What if I had parked near the Murrah Building, or walked past it going for a cup of coffee? What if I'd been on time for work?"

Troy: "I'd like to say I'm happy and upbeat about life, but I have to tell you, Roy, that I'm very angry that I have an 18-month-old and a 7-month-old who will have to grow up in a world with hijackings and tragedy and terror. But I'll never forget my sister and what she did."

I asked Troy if there was anything more he wanted to say about his sister.

"I just want everyone to know that my sister was there, that she did her job," he said. "Without her, I don't know that I would ever have been able to comprehend April 19. We went to the memorial service and I remember saying to myself, 'My sister is a hero. She's my hero.'"

Mom and Dad

Regina and Bernard Firestone...
Their light still shines on me.

chapter
28

DANCING UNDER THE STARS

You've heard the term "incurable romantic." That was my dad, and he never wanted to be cured.

To some, romance is an illusion, a fabrication that, when held up to the light, proves flimsy and one-dimensional and fake. Not to my dad. Damn the cynics and the apologists. My father didn't live a day in his life without a sense of romance. To him that would not be living.

Nearly everything he did, every word he spoke, was somehow anchored in romance. Every song that mattered to him was about romance. Every book and play and turn of a phrase he enjoyed had something to do with romance.

For him, truth was the long kiss, the dance under the stars, the magic of believing in something that seems impossibly lost for so many of us.

Romance was easy to find. He found it in black-and-white movies. In names from the past. Spencer Tracy, Katharine Hepburn, William Powell, Myrna Loy. And in the names of thousands of actors in thousands of movies, people he could pick out in the background and whose names he could recite from memory. Useless information? Maybe, to most. But for my dad there was romance in remembering people that time forgot.

He was happy in the past. You can talk about war, depression, segregation and other terrible things we've tried to put behind us. He really believed that the past had more glory, more honor, and, above all, more romance.

My dad and mom were not perfect, but they were a perfect fit. What was true and powerful was their love. They were so complimentary, and not always because of the spoken compliment, though there were thousands of those.

How hard it often seems to follow their example. It seems so daunting, so impossible. A tough act to follow, because there are no second acts. When she walked into a room, he always heard violins. Sometimes they were loud and sweeping, sometimes quiet, but they were always there.

When he walked through a doorway, she knew instinctively what kind of day he had had. She believed her life was about him.

They were not without conflict, but not a day went by when they didn't love one another in word or deed. And when she left, he tried to show his strength, his bravado. His performance fooled us all. In the end, though, no one could replace his one true romance, and so he soon let go and joined her.

What do we remember when we speak of my father? We remember his commitment. Every day, in every way, he tried to do the right thing for his family. He didn't always succeed. Sometimes his words, actions, gestures, hurt us. But he never, ever, wouldn't, couldn't live with malice towards anyone. That's not in a romantic's makeup.

There were times he confounded us, annoyed us, confused us. But those moments were always overshadowed by his basic goodness. He never harbored a hateful thought. How I wish I could say that about myself.

What does he leave me and my siblings and my children? Something more profound and enduring than riches. He leaves us the lessons of a man of true honor.

No child went unloved. No family member lacked the experience of being made to feel as if they were the most important person in the room.

And this from a man who found it hard to say the simple words, "I love you."

He tried to teach us that striving for love, loyalty and romance made for a worthy and worthwhile life.

When John Lennon died, on my birthday, even though my dad didn't appreciate rock music he wrote me a beautiful and compassionate letter. He understood my sorrow, because he felt the same way about his music, and because my hurt was his.

I'm not sure how we endured the initial months of grieving when he left, but we did, we shined through. And we did it because my mother and father still shine upon us, the glow of their laugher, cheer and infinite kindness.

They are waltzing together now, somewhere in the stars, to a thousand violins, because true love never dies.

With Warren Sapp

With Ray Lewis

Their bark is worse than their bite...Thank goodness!

DANGEROUS DUDES

I'm not going to go all Father Flanagan on you here, but I want to tell you the story of two football players with bad reputations, and both of them are welcome on my show and in my life, any time.

Ray Lewis was involved in a murder. Warren Sapp was involved with drugs and has been accused of thuggery and buffoonery.

Are they bad guys? The older I get, the harder it is to make that kind of black-and-white call. If my experience has taught me anything, it's that you can't judge a book by its cover or a man's character by his news clippings.

Critics might say, "There goes Roy, putting a good-guy label on two bad guys because they're great athletes who will sit down with him on his show."

Lewis and Sapp are great athletes and they are willing and interesting guests, but I hope my judgments aren't that simplistic. Let me tell you about these two.

Ray Lewis is perhaps the greatest linebacker of the past decade, one of the true impact players in the NFL, maybe the most ferocious man in the maniacal game. He admits he comes from a long line of thugs. He told me, "I was raised by thugs. Thugs were the only ones who loved me when I was growing up. My father was a thug."

When Lewis was in high school, his father ran out on him, told Ray he would be back but he didn't come back, and Ray learned he could always count on his father to lie to him and to let him down.

Ray went to college at Miami and was an instant star. During his junior year, his roommate, a player named Marlin Barnes, was bludgeoned to death in their apartment in what police believed to be a drug-related homicide. When Lewis returned to the apartment it was swarming with police and splattered with blood, and Ray figures he would have been murdered, too, had he been home at the time.

Lewis was drafted in '96 in the first round by the Baltimore Ravens and was immediately successful. He has been named Defensive Player of the Year twice (as of this writing). But Lewis was raised in a violent world and fell into that world again just after the 2000 Super Bowl in Atlanta, after his fourth season in the league. Two men were murdered outside the Cobalt Lounge in Atlanta after a Super Bowl party. There was a scuffle, the two men were stabbed repeatedly, and Lewis and some other people jumped into their nearby limo and sped away.

For the next 48 hours Ray Lewis was a fugitive, wanted on suspicion of murder. On TV, the victims' parents were announcing, "Ray Lewis killed my son."

This was not a good time for an NFL player to be in the crime news. The O.J. Simpson case was still fresh in people's minds, Ray Caruth's pregnant girlfriend had been murdered with his involvement, Fred Lane had been killed with a bullet, and Mark Chumura stood accused of raping his babysitter.

Lewis was arrested just as he was about to board a jet to Hawaii to play in the Pro Bowl. He admitted that he had been drunk the night of the murder. He told me he never owned a knife in his life and hadn't been in a fight since high school, and he felt he was a victim of guilt by association, but he admitted he had made a poor choice in the company he was keeping.

Lewis spent fifteen days in a jail cell. He was only allowed to accept collect calls, and one call was from his son, five-year-old

Ray-Ray, who asked him, "Daddy, why were you on TV wearing chains?"

Ray didn't know what to say, so he told his son it was all a joke. Then he remembered how his father had lied to him, and Ray fell apart, sobbing.

To keep his sanity he worked out – 1,500 push-ups and 500 sit-ups every night. The jail guards had him on a suicide watch, so they would wake him up all during the night. Then he was placed in an isolation cell in a ward for psychotic prisoners. Day and night there was screaming, yelling, singing and weird noises, a mini version of hell.

Lewis hadn't been tried yet, but he felt as if he had been convicted and sentenced. The NFL fined him $250,000, the largest fine in league history.

He plea-bargained, pleading guilty to obstruction of justice and agreeing to testify against two of the men he was with that night. Initially Lewis had withheld information about the two men from the police, a misguided throwback to the old thug code – never rat on a friend. Lewis was remorseful.

He got back to football but with a new reputation. Every time he emerged from an arena tunnel before a game, fans would yell, "Hey, Ray, you gonna murder someone today? You gonna stab someone?" "Look, son, it's Jeffrey Dahmer."

Ray said he resolved to turn all that anger, hate and negative energy into something positive. He would become involved in the community, and not just by writing a few checks and playing in charity golf tournaments. He would use his celebrity and even his bad reputation to help others.

I spent three days with Lewis while taping an extended interview, and every day he spoke to a different large group of kids, explaining how you can mess up your life just by hanging out with the wrong people.

I was impressed. His talks seemed sincere and he definitely captured the attention of his audience.

People ask me, who are the good guys and who are the bad guys? I'm not going to tell you Ray Lewis is the quintessential good guy, but I will tell you that he made a decision to renounce his thug life, and to use his experiences and his fame or infamy to reach out and help others. In the face of much public ridicule and abuse, he chose to become vocal and active, rather than angry and reclusive.

I admire Ray Lewis for that. Before our interview I knew him only by reputation, and honestly I was wary of dealing with him. But I found him to be thoughtful and not without a sense of humor. To me he seemed a man who has acknowledged mistakes and is trying to make a difference.

One year after his arrest and humiliation, Lewis led his Ravens to a Super Bowl title and was named MVP of the game.

* * *

Warren Sapp is another guy I admire and enjoy being around. Like Lewis, Sapp took a reputation that had been dragged through the gutter and turned it around. Both of these guys, in fact, have gone from being outlaws, literally, to being poster guys for the NFL.

Sapp hit the skids before he ever got near the NFL. Like Lewis, Warren played college ball at Miami, and was projected to be a very high first-round pick. However, a day or two before the draft, ESPN's Chris Mortensen reported that Sapp's stock had dropped because he had tested positive for drugs on one or more occasions while at Miami.

The entire Sapp clan had gathered to watch the glorious draft telecast. They all saw the ESPN report. They turned to Warren and said, "You did all that?"

"Now I ain't never been a choir boy," Sapp told me, "I never held myself up to be anybody role model, but I know that I never ever tested positive or used cocaine. I could be a complete idiot to use cocaine anywhere near a scouting combine, so Chris Mortensen was an outright liar. He lied about me testing positive for cocaine and for multiple times testing positive for marijuana, although I never denied that I used marijuana.

"I've been an idiot all my life. I was a C or below-C student, so in many people's minds I might be an academic idiot, but I'm not an idiot of the street. What Chris Mortensen did was to destroy me and destroy my career without getting the facts straight."

Partly because of that report, Sapp's stock did plummet and he wasn't drafted until the No. 12 spot in the first round. So the report/rumor hurt him financially, but it also cost him heavily in terms of respect and reputation.

But if we fast-forward through the first few years of his career, we find Sapp establishing himself as a star defensive lineman (voted to six consecutive Pro Bowls) and a respected man.

There has been controversy. Sapp was warned by the league for running through the opposing team's pre-game warm-up area. He was fined $50,000 after accidentally bumping and knocking down an official. And in '02 he set of a national debate when, on an interception runback, he leveled Green Bay's Chad Clifton, sending Clifton to the hospital with a serious pelvic injury.

Sapp has never been one to say, "No comment," so he's often in the news. So he is controversial. But a respected man and player? Absolutely.

I told Sapp that his style of play reminded me of Deacon Jones, a Hall of Fame defensive end for the old Los Angeles Rams.

"Funny you should say that," Sapp said, "because I'm from a small town outside of Orlando, and Deacon Jones is from a small town outside of Orlando. We both came from absolute poverty. He went to a tiny college in South Carolina and I went to Miami, but when we came out of college, neither of us were respected.

"I swear whenever they photographed Deacon, they made him look darker, because all you ever see is his eyes and his teeth. Same with me. I wear cornrows, people never see me smile, they only see me scowl. So you know what I'm going to do? I'm going to let them have their stereotype. Whenever they take a picture of me I'm going to scowl and give 'em the mean eyes, and I'm going to play their game and I'm going to be the athlete they tried to portray me to be, and I'm just gonna play my ass off."

Sapp said he wanted to play so well that no matter what people thought him to be, they would have to accept him. He wanted achieve the power status of a George Steinbrenner or Mark Cuban, where you are so absolutely successful that you can be what you want to be and you're no longer a fool, you're colorful, an eccentric, a rebel. If you're a failure and a fool, you're just a fool.

Sapp is a black man who makes it clear that he never forgets the color of his skin or how that color affects the way he is treated in life. When he was fined for knocking down the official, Sapp said, "It's a slave system."

Arthur Ashe once told me that being a black person in America is like having a pebble in your shoe. To some people it's painful or annoying, while others try to ignore it and just keep going.

"When I walk onto an airplane with my first-class ticket," Sapp said, "when they're calling for first-class to board the plane and I'm standing in line, they look at you and they say, 'It's first class only.' 'See, I can read. I know that it says first class.'"

Sapp was offended when he dined at a top restaurant in Tampa and ordered lamb chops.

"Now, every man in America knows what you get with lamb chops, correct? You get mint jelly, right? And they said, 'Do you want some barbecue sauce with that?' And I said, 'Yeah, and I want some watermelon and some Kool-Aid too.'"

We talked about what might have been Sapp's most memorable game, a Monday Night Football game against Brett Favre and the Packers in Green Bay, and Favre and Sapp were the stars of the show. Warren sacked Favre three or four times and the cameras caught them jawing at one another, nose to nose, seemingly almost coming to blows.

"I'd sack Favre and he'd pop back up, say, 'Get off me!' and push me and I'd push him back. I love Brett Favre, I love him because he's a quarterback version of me. He was a no-good, broken-down, stoned-out country boy, and I was a no-good, broken-down, stoned-out ghetto boy."

Then Warren told me about an incident that occurred the night of that game on the plane flight back to Tampa. He said he was feeling really good about the game he had just played, he was looking out the window, it was dark but he could see some clouds.

"For some reason, I flashed on my brother," Sapp said. "I've never really talked about him. He was the guy who never made it, who back in the ghetto and was always trying to push me to be better than running with these gangs and being around the wrong people. He was always pushing me."

His brother had a massive heart attack and died in his early 30s.

"At that moment, looking out the window of the plane and at the clouds I said, 'This is probably as close as I'll ever be to you.' And I have just come off one of my best games, while at the same time, I was brought back to earth by the fact that my brother didn't have a chance to see this, and I swore to him that I'd make something of myself, and for my family. He never had a chance to see my success, just like I never had a chance for my father to see it. But somehow, some way, I know I'm making him proud, and I will never forget who I am. I'm black, I'll never be white, I'll never bow to anybody, never allow myself to be marketed as anything other than who I am. I'll make a name for myself in spite of what they say about me."

And Sapp has done that. He led Tampa Bay to a Super Bowl championship in '02.

Warren Sapp and Ray Lewis became two of the billboard faces of the NFL, in promos and advertising, and in images of excellence. A cynic might say it's all about the end result and about celebrity, that a corporation would put Hitler on the cover of a football video game if he could tackle.

I choose to believe that Sapp and Lewis are examples of people who, through hard work and strong will, have overcome and risen above.

Are they perfect gentlemen? No, but sometimes it's not about sorting people into bins – good guy, bad guy. Sometimes it's about character.

With Buck O'Neil

The toughest softie I ever met.

chapter 30

NO TIME FOR HATE

The most stubborn person I've ever met in sports was Buck O'Neil.

The man could not take a hint.

When he was a youngster, he couldn't attend high school because of his color, and then he wasn't allowed into college, same reason. So Buck got his education elsewhere, earned himself the life-experience equivalent of several doctorates.

Buck was a fine baseball player, but society wouldn't let him play in the major leagues. So he played in the Negro Leagues, and had himself a fine career, playing and managing, embodying the skill, pride and dignity of the black players of his day, and mocking the racist exclusivity of the "big" leagues.

Buck should have been bitter, but he was stubborn, he held out against bitterness his whole life. His wife Ora Lee died in 1997 after a 15-year battle with cancer, which Buck called "the greatest 15 years of my life," because they had grown even closer. Bitter? Buck would speak at fight-cancer benefits and sing, a capella, "I Believe."

When baseball's color barriers began falling, baseball still wouldn't let Buck manage in the big leagues because baseball wasn't ready for a black manager. But Buck wouldn't go away, he became the first black major league coach, with the Cubs in '62, and a scout.

And all along he honed his greatest skill: touching, inspiring, teaching and entertaining people. And in the final analysis he was the greatest ambassador the game has ever had. I'm not talking about the black game. I'm talking about the game.

All of that wasn't good enough for a special committee that in 2006 selected heroes from the Negro Leagues for induction into the Baseball Hall of Fame. The committee found 17 players, managers and executives worthy of the great honor, but Buck fell one vote short. Political infighting revolving around Kansas City's Negro League Museum, which Buck helped create and build, probably cost him that final honor.

His response to the snub was surprising only if you didn't know Buck.

"God's been good to me," he told a couple hundred well-wishers the day the vote was announced. "They didn't think Buck was good enough to be in the Hall of Fame. That's the way they thought about it and that's the way it is, so we're going to live with that. Now, if I'm a Hall of Famer for you, that's all right with me. Just keep loving old Buck. Don't weep for Buck. No, man, be happy, be thankful."

Buck O'Neil died later that year, at 94. Some might say he died of a broken heart, but my theory is that Buck got called up to a higher league, and they rolled out the red carpet to the Hall of Fame, and Buck was carried in on the shoulders of the men for whom he was a teammate, a leader, a mentor, and an example of how to play ball and how to live life.

One of Buck's beautiful talents was storytelling. He was a marvelous oral historian of the Negro Leagues, his mind sharp and his stories lively until the very end.

Here's a story Buck liked to tell, especially at a time when every pitcher in baseball (and every manager) was deathly afraid to pitch to Barry Bonds. That wouldn't have happened when he played, Buck said, in this story printed in *Esquire* magazine:

> *It was the second game of the (Negro League) World Series. We're playing at Pittsburgh. We're ahead 2-0 in the seventh inning, and Satchel Paige is on the mound. Batter knocks a triple down the left-field line. I go over to the mound and Satchel says, 'You know what I'm fixin' to do?' And I said, 'You're gonna get this guy out and we goin' home.' He said, 'No, I'm gonna walk him. I'm gonna walk the next guy, too, and pitch to Josh Gibson.' Fill the bases to get to the great Josh Gibson! I said, 'Man, don't be facetious.' I call out the manager: 'Listen to what this fool is sayin'!' And the manager says, 'All these people in the ballpark came out here to see Satchel Paige and Josh Gibson. Let him do what he wants to do.'*
>
> *Now there's some history here. See, years before, Satchel and Josh played for the same team, and they had this conversation as they were travelin' through the Blue Mountain. Satchel told Josh: 'They say you're the best hitter in the world, and I know I'm the best pitcher. One day we're gonna meet up on different teams and see who the best really is.'*
>
> *So Satchel walks the first batter, and as he's walking the second he's having a conversation with Josh in the on-deck circle, saying, 'Remember that time in the Blue Mountains?' As Josh heads to the plate, the crowd's feeling it, but Satchel isn't through yet. Oh, no. He's just setting the stage. He sets his glove on the mound and motions for the trainer, Jewbaby Floyd.*
>
> *Now it's show time. Jewbaby goes out to the mound with a glass foaming over with bicarbonate of soda. Understand, Satchel was famous for having stomach problems. So Satchel drinks that glass down and lets out a great belch. Big old belch! 'Okay, Josh,' he says. 'You ready?' So Josh steps into the batter's box with that great, great body after two guys were walked just to get to him. And it was scary. All you could do was hope he didn't kill someone. Satchel throws him a*

fastball. Josh doesn't even move his bat. Strike one. 'Okay, Josh, now I'm gonna throw you another fastball, just about the same place,' Satchel says. 'But it's gonna be a little harder than the last one.'

Josh doesn't move his bat. Strike two! 'I got you oh-and-two, and in this league I'm supposed to knock you down. But I'm not gonna throw smoke at yo' yoke. I'm gonna throw a pea at yo' knee.' Now, Satchel is about six-four, but when he wound up and kicked that leg up, he looked seven feet tall. Josh never even swung. Strike three! And let me tell you, when Satchel walked off the mound he was ten feet tall. He said, 'Nobody hits Satchel's fastball.'

You know, I must have told that story a million times. But I never get tired of it. Why would I? Every time I tell it, I'm thirty years old again, playing in the World Series.

I emceed a function in Kansas City a few years ago, where Buck was the honored guest. In his honor I sang "You Make Me Feel So Young." As I began to sing, the crowd of 1,000 people suddenly started cheering wildly. I was puzzled, then I turned around and saw Buck dancing, by himself, as I sang. It was a priceless moment.

At the end of that evening, Buck addressed the crowd and said: "Folks, I want all of you to hold hands. That's what I'm asking you to do tonight, for old Buck. All of you, hold hands, and repeat after me: 'The greatest thing in all my life... is loving you. The greatest thing in all my life... is loving you.' "

I believe we owe a debt to Buck O'Neil for what he gave us, and the only way we can repay that debt it is to live our lives in the pursuit of love and happiness.

Buck was more than just a wonderfully entertaining fellow. He was a philosopher, a man with great wisdom. But stubborn to the end, there's one thing he refused to learn.

"I never learned to hate," Buck said.

With Shaquille O'Neal

With Charles Barkley and Hakeem Olajuwon

Shaq, Barkley and Hakeem – Bigger than life.

A BOX OF CHOCOLATES

Nuggets of wit, wisdom and whimsy from over the years.

* * *

I asked Shaquille O'Neal to describe the difference between his personality and Kobe Bryant's.

"Well," Shaq said, "Kobe is a loner. And me, I'm a socialist."

* * *

Andre Agassi submitted to my phrase-association test.

Roy: "Match point at Wimbledon Centre Court."

Agassi: "It's quiet, it's a very peaceful moment, it's like all you ever saw that whole day was the tennis ball. And it's just you and the ball, it's quite a good feeling. The only sense you have is feel, and it's internal. It's not ears, eyes, it's not taste. It's feel, it's like your body when you're about to get shot-you know you're about to win the championship."

Roy: "Agassi at age 29 vs. Agassi at age 21."

Agassi: "(As a 29-year-old) I would tell myself, 'You know what? He hasn't learned how to hang in there and believe in himself in the most important times, so hang in there long enough.'"

Roy: "The thing I've come to realize and accept."

Agassi: "Always choose the hard road."

* * *

Charles Barkley and Hakeem Olajuwon were on the show together. Hakeem is from Lagos, Nigeria, he speaks five languages and all of them softly. He's a devout and humble Muslin. Charming and ebullient personality, but he is almost always serious.

Charles is Charles.

I asked them if they believe they are going to heaven.

"Well," Hakeem said, "service to Allah is the most important thing, whatever I do is in service to Allah, my performance as a player and human being. If I serve Allah with devotion, perhaps I will go to heaven."

"What about you?" I said to Charles. "Will you go to heaven?"

"I don't know," he said, "but it's gonna be a close vote."

* * *

Barkley and I were discussing whether or not it was kosher of the Lakers to announce that they were listening to offers for Shaq O'Neal.

I said, "The guy's costing the Lakers $30 million. What's wrong with saying they'll listen to offers?"

Barkley: "Roy, you're married, am I right? Would you like to hear your wife on TV say, 'I'm listening to offers for Roy'?"

* * *

Shannon Sharpe, former tight end for the Broncos, is a very sharp cookie, but he had what you might call an undistinguished academic career at Savannah State. I asked him, "Shannon, would you say you matriculated to the level of *magna cum laude*?"

Sharpe replied, "Roy, the fact that I even graduated is *Thank you, Lordie.*"

* * *

Michael Irvin talked about the play that ended his career, a hit that left him lying on the grass, temporarily paralyzed from the neck down.

"What I remember, Roy, is going down, turning over and landing on my back, trying to get my mouthpiece out of my mouth. 'Just get up! Get up!' The tough guy in me come out. But all I could do was close my eyes.

"I'm like, 'I know this is not happening.' All I could think about was my family. I thought about when I was getting dressed for that trip, putting my cuff links in and my little boy Michael, he just wanted to play. He steps in front of me like he's Deion (Sanders), and I'm trying to get off the jam while I put my cufflinks in, and my wife says, 'You better go, you're gonna miss the plane.' I'm telling Michael, 'We'll play when I get back, we'll play when I get back.'

"All those years you're just running, running, running, always think you'll have time to do stuff later. 'I got time to play later, do it later.' I lay on that carpet, I was thinking, 'That's it, I'll never have time to play with my kid.' All I could see was the sky. I was prayin' as hard as I could pray. I was as scared as I could be."

I asked Irvin what he misses most about playing football.

"The thing I miss most is Troy (Aikman) just looking at me, third-and-nine, and saying, 'Man, I'm throwin' it to you no matter what, go and get it.' And going to get it for him, not because he's the quarterback for the Dallas Cowboys, but because he's my boy.

"They (the defenders) got a nine-man front and Emmitt (Smith) looking at me and saying, 'They got nine men, you got one-on-one, you gotta go get it so I can get mine.' It was bigger than football. They were my boys.

"Take the money, take it all. That's what I miss, is them saying, 'I'm counting on you.'"

* * *

Abe Lemmons, the late great Oklahoma basketball coach, told about the time he got a technical foul, then the ref blew another call and Abe was just livid.

Lemmons (in his down-home drawl): "I said, 'Hey, ref, come over here a second. You know, if I get a second technical, I'm thrown out of the gym, right?' He said, 'That's right.' 'Let me ask you this. Would you give me a technical for something I'm thinkin'?' The ref says, 'No.' I say, 'Good, because I'm thinking you're a sunuvabitch.'"

* * *

The first time I met Wilt Chamberlain was in 1979, in Santa Monica. I came out of a restaurant and saw him in a white convertible Bentley, top down. In the back seat were two great danes that look like small horses. Wilt's passenger was a blonde stuffed into a tiny leather dress. Wilt was wearing a brief, leopard skin bathing suit, purple coat, Buster-Brown velveteen cap with a feather, and wraparound shades. He's got his bare feet propped on the steering wheel.

I walked up, introduced myself, told him I'd love to have him on my show.

He said, "Roy, I know who you are and I like your show. But you have to understand, I try to keep a low profile."

* * *

Wilt did come on the show, many times. One day we were talking about Bill Russell, Chamberlain's great rival and friend. And Wilt was a very intelligent and glib guy, but he got stuck for a word... aura.

He said, "Every time I took the court against Russell, got in the paint with him, I was impressed and inspired and overwhelmed by his undeniable... uh...you know...uh...*aroma*."

* * *

I always felt it was a shame that Wilt bragged in his last book that he bedded 20,000 women. That page obliterated the rest of the book, which was pretty good and which Wilt wrote himself. In the athletic world, a star jock writing his own book is as amazing as 20,000 bedmates.

But we talked about the 20,000 and Wilt said, "It was never a conquest. It was a mutual consent, where our minds both wanted something and our bodies did it. Many of them are my friends today. I could remember maybe 15,000 of them by name, and the rest, if I saw them I'd remember them."

* * *

Harmon Killebrew tells great baseball stories, has a wonderful memory.

"We were playing the Tigers in June of '55, Billy Hoeft pitching for them," Killebrew said. "Frank House was catching and he said, 'Kid, we're going to throw you a fastball.' I was 18, I didn't know if he was telling the truth. It was a fastball and I hit it 476 feet. I trotted around the bases and as I touched home, Frank House said, 'Kid, that's the last time we're ever going to tell you.'"

* * *

Kurt Warner remains one of the rags-to-riches success stories in sport. He went from stocking shelves in a supermarket in South Dakota after college, to leading the Rams to a Super Bowl title and winning two NFL MVP awards.

"Yeah, Cedar Falls, at the Hy-Vee Food Store," Warner said, "workin' the late shift, and you're putting the boxes up on the shelves. And you're tellin' everybody that you're gonna play in the National Football League. And you believe it."

I asked, "Did people ever try to talk you down, did they think you were crazy?"

Warner said, "No, they never really talked me down, but you know how you get into those situations where you claim something and you can just tell people are just kinda, you know, goin' with it, but shakin' their head, goin' 'No way, this guy's workin' in a supermarket.'

"They usually asked me what the prospects were, if I heard from any teams or talked to anybody. You could just kinda get the feelin' that in the back of their mind they thought it was pretty far-fetched that a guy working in the *supermarket* more than two years outta college was actually gonna be playin' in the NFL some day."

* * *

Warren Sapp told this high school story:

"I hid my progress report card, my mid-term, I folded it up and hid it. Got it in a good hidin' spot. But you know, your mother always knows a little more than you did. She found it. I knew I hid it in a good spot, too, Roy. But she found it and she stormed out there to the football field, and I looked up and said, 'Oh, shit, here she comes.'

"And my boy looked and me and said, 'Here *who* comes?' I said, 'My mamma.' And she was stompin' across the field."

I asked, "Did she talk to the coach?"

"Went straight to him. Straight to him. Said, 'Get him and tell him to come over here.'"

"That's your mom," I said.

"Yeah," Sapp said, "that's why I love her to death."

* * *

Marshall Faulk talked about growing up in a rough section of New Orleans.

"Oh, I've seen people get shot right next to me. I'm talking about not just once, I'm talkin' about shot to where the guy walks over to him and continues to shoot him. I'm talking about 13,14 shots, this in daytime, comin' home from school."

* * *

Keyshawn Johnson was shot in the butt and ankle during a drive-by shooting in Los Angeles when he was a teenager. I asked him what it felt like. He smiled.

"Ah," Johnson said, "it's a little fun, it's a tingling, warm, scary sensation for a minute, until you find out you're gonna be all right, and then you're cool. Then you're just mad."

* * *

Barry Switzer's father was a loan shark and bootlegger.

"I loved my daddy," Switzer said. "He was a strong man's-man, men loved my dad because he took care of people. He took care of people in the black community, he had a lot of black people working for him.

"At the same time, he was a tough, rough guy, he always carried a pistol on him. I've seen him pull the pistol a lot of times, I've seen him arrested, handcuffed. I've seen him beaten. When I was a small child, I'd go to the state penitentiary to visit him. We'd drive up on Sundays. Our eyes would make contact, then we'd glance away like we hadn't seen each other. We were both embarrassed to be there."

* * *

Hubie Brown is a coach's coach. If I wanted to learn to coach, I would sit at Hubie's feet and absorb pearls of wisdom, such as:

. "I always say this, you've got to have style. You cannot give me your best coach, your best teacher, without telling me that they have a distinct style. They are not worrying about what anybody else is doing. See, they are innovators. They're risk takers."

- "You're not going to have a good team in the NBA unless your best two guys are coachable. When your two best guys are coachable, you can get the job done, because they will work at practice. They accept what you are trying to do from a philosophical standpoint, and the rest of the guys will fall in line like sheep."

- On what a coach should not say: "Stop saying that the players don't have to be accountable. Stop saying that they don't have to work to their potential, because you want to be loved. When you're a teacher, it's your job to take that talent and strain its potential until it cries for mercy. You owe it to them."

* * *

Nolan Ryan asked me to emcee the gala opening of his Nolan Ryan Center in Alvin, Texas.

The Center includes a full-on museum, which has a Hall of Baseballs... 5,714 of them hanging on the walls, like paintings in the Louvre. Each ball represents a Ryan strikeout, and each has a plaque with the name of the whiff victim. Ryan, who is one of the absolute sweetest and most genuine men you'll ever meet, gave me a tour.

"You know, Roy," he said, "I struck out Roger Maris and Mark McGwire. I struck out 45 fathers and sons."

He pointed to a plaque that reads, "Claudell Washington, 48." I asked him, "Did Washington wear No. 48?"

Ryan said, "No, that's how many times I struck him out."

Nolan is a banker and cattle rancher. We sat down for dinner and they served massive slabs of beef, like something Fred Flintstone would order. They served me one that must have weighed five pounds. I don't eat meat, but I felt foolish telling Ryan that, since we were on a beef ranch in the heart of Texas. It's like telling a Texan you drive an electric car. So I told him I never eat before I perform, but I'd take it with me for later.

"Are you sure?" he said. "Because that's Eloise."

"What do you mean?" I asked.

"That's Eloise. She was with our herd for six years."

Ryan's the only guy I've ever dined with who was on a first-name basis with the beef he was eating.

When it was time to leave, Nolan thanked me and handed me a paper bag dripping with grease. Eloise.

* * *

On the first day of the O.J. Simpson trial, the jury was sequestered and Judge Lance Ito was deciding what could and could not be admitted as evidence. One piece of potential evidence that the prosecution wanted entered was a videotape of Simpson being interviewed on my show, talking about having an altercation with his wife.

Simpson's attorney Johnnie Cochran objected, he said, "This is an interview with Roy Firestone, your honor. This isn't Mike Wallace, this is *Roy Firestone*, he has no credibility at all!"

One of the most-watched moments in television history.

"Thanks a lot, Johnnie!" I yelled at my TV.

With Steve Young

One guy who's got it all figured out.

chapter

32

THE MOMENT OF IMPACT

When Steve Young graduated from Brigham Young University in 1984 as the hottest college quarterback in the country, a pro football war was raging.

The NFL was being challenged by the upstart United States Football League. After a bidding war, Young signed with the USFL's Los Angeles Express for $40 million.

What does a kid just out of college do with that kind of money? If the kid is Steve Young, nothing. He rented a cheap, unfurnished apartment, drove a beat-up car and bought no new clothes.

His roommate would find uncashed six-figure paychecks behind the couch cushions.

The "problem" for Steve was that he was raised to believe a person's worth and character are not measured in dollars. Young couldn't reconcile his income with his output of services rendered to society. He couldn't convince himself that he was worth 400 times the salary paid to a schoolteacher or social worker.

Young isn't cheap, he simply never got the hang of spending money. During his 49er career, one San Francisco writer noted that "Steve Young, in the course of his career, has squandered dozens of dollars."

The last time I saw Steve he was driving a Toyota Prius, and, long since retired from football, he was begging for (okay, *raising*) money for his Forever Young Foundation, which promotes the health, development and protection of at-risk children.

Steve Young is the most unsuperstar-like superstar you will ever meet. He's as pretentious and self-important as the guy who delivers your pizza. When you talk to Steve, for 10 seconds or an hour, you have his complete attention and interest. He doesn't just listen or talk, he connects. You are his buddy.

Young views life on simple terms. He once told me that while he has never read the book, he believes in the concept that everything you need to know in life you learned in kindergarten.

Teamwork, for instance. Young led the 49ers to victory in Super Bowl XXIX in 1995, and described to me the feeling.

"There's nothing like the moment when you're in the locker room, right after the Super Bowl," he said. "It's quiet, you kneel down, say the Lord's Prayer, 50 guys, no media, fans are outside, you're the champions, and there's a moment when you finish the prayer, you stand up and you look at each other. I'll never forget that, for about 15 seconds everybody just stares at one another, we couldn't believe we were the champions of the world. To share that moment with so many other human beings."

I attended the Pro Football Hall of Fame induction ceremony in 2005 when Young was enshrined. His speech was poetry, absolutely beautiful, delivered it from notes he scrawled longhand, like Abe Lincoln at Gettysburg.

Young talked of faith, saying, "I used to hold on to the ball despite the fact that my receiver was open, because I couldn't see him. I'm a lot shorter than Dan (Marino, fellow enshrinee), many times the big linemen blocked my view. It was (coach) Mike Holmgren who yelled at me one game and said, 'Jerry (Rice) was open. Why didn't you throw it to him?' I said, 'I couldn't see him.' 'Well, you better start seeing him.' Thanks for the tip. I'll be sure to start seeing what I can't see as soon as I see it.

"But it made me pause. Maybe it would be good for my career if I just threw it where I thought my receiver was. I had just seen him a second ago, I knew where he was headed. Throw it. Simple. Go on faith and knowledge."

The part of Young's speech that really grabbed me was about "the moment of impact." He was talking about football, but I think he would agree that what he said applies to life.

"No career, no matter how great, is smooth all the way thorough," Young told the audience. "But one thing is sure: if you are lucky enough to make it a career, you cannot play very long without a love of the game. The game demands too much of you physically, emotionally and even spiritually to stay in it if you don't love it. I don't care how much you get paid, you show me a 6-8-10-year veteran of the NFL and I'll show you a man that loves the game.

"Money isn't the key at the moment of impact. I have seen a lot of guys play for money in practice and warm-ups, but I have never seen one play for money at the point of contact."

That's why I believe that sports matter, because we all face moments of impact. We face a crisis or a crossroads or an opportunity, a situation where money can't bail us out, where phoniness or procrastination are useless tools. That's when love, faith, character and courage kick in.

People like Steve Young, Dikembe Mutombo, Andre Agassi, Magic Johnson, they show us what can be done at the moment of impact, in the arena and beyond.

They are quiet heroes, they do their most spectacular work when the crowds are gone.

That's why I believe sports matter.